DONALYN MILLER & COLB'

THE COMMONSENSE GUIDE TO YOUR
CLASSROOM LIBRARY

Building a Collection That Inspires, Engages, and Challenges Readers

■SCHOLASTIC

Senior Vice President and Publisher: Tara Welty
Acquisitions Editor: Lois Bridges
Editorial Director: Sarah Longhi
Development Editor: Raymond Coutu
Senior Editor: Shelley Griffin
Production Editor: Danny Miller
Creative Director: Tannaz Fassihi
Interior Designer: Maria Lilja

Scholastic is not responsible for the content of third-party websites and does not endorse any site or imply that the information on the site is error-free, correct, accurate, or reliable.

Cover illustration: Erin Robinson
All photos courtesy of Colby Sharp.

Additional credits ©: 58: "Volume Conference Form" from *Intervention Reinvention* copyright © 2021 by Stephanie Harvey, Annie Ward, Maggie Hoddinott, and Suzanne Carroll. Published by Scholastic Inc. Used by permission; 96: Excerpt from "Elementary Reading Attitude Survey" from "Measuring Attitude Toward Reading: A New Tool for Teachers" by Dennis J. Kear and Michael C. McKenna, from *The Reading Teacher,* volume 43. Copyright © 1990 by International Reading Association. Used by permission of John Wiley & Sons, Inc.
All rights reserved.

ISBN 978-1-338-77518-1

1 2 3 4 5 6 7 8 9 10   40   31 30 29 28 27 26 25 24 23 22

Scholastic Inc., 557 Broadway, New York, NY 10012

CONTENTS

INTRODUCTION

No matter how long you've taught young readers, it is impossible to predict or imagine the leaps in understanding that can happen when a school year (or two) doesn't go as planned. The COVID-19 pandemic changed teaching and learning in unimaginable ways, but it gave many educators deeper insight into the resources and mindsets kids need to learn and thrive. What have we learned during the pandemic that shapes our work with students going forward? How can shifts in classroom and school conditions influence long-term support for readers?

One School Year Ends...

Every teacher has their own story to tell about teaching and caring for students during the COVID-19 pandemic. So many classroom routines and instructional methods changed out of necessity. School communities focused on connecting with families and supporting learning online at home. In many schools, engaging readers became more challenging because of reduced book access. Worried teachers and librarians limited access to books to keep kids safe, which was concerning because the link between access to reading materials and engagement with reading has been well-documented (Miller & Sharp, 2018).

Because Colby's students at Parma Elementary in Parma, Michigan, could not use the school or classroom libraries in the same ways to find books and forge relationships around reading, they were not as engaged. Most of all, it took much longer for Colby to connect kids with books and with each other.

Reflecting on what worked to build community and support literacy development, Colby focused on the rituals, routines, and instructional moves that provided time and space for students to engage in authentic literacy activities—daily independent reading and writing, read-alouds and book talks, and frequent chances to read, write, and talk with their classmates about what they were reading and studying. Colby worked to get books into kids' hands that they could read and enjoy, but there were obstacles to book access that he couldn't control.

COVID restrictions prevented students from visiting the school library for regular checkouts. So, the school librarian, Ms. Madden, came by once a week with books on a cart. She brought tubs containing nonfiction, graphic novels, and other books of interest. If kids asked for a specific book, she would bring it the following week. Students used hand sanitizer when handling books, and browsing was limited to one child at a time.

Enter the Classroom Library

The classroom library, typically the heart of the classroom community, was severely restricted. Kids could not congregate in it, dig in the bins, or pass books around. Colby could not dip into the classroom library during reading conferences to grab books. Spontaneous interactions with books and conversations about them between students occurred infrequently. Without regular opportunities to engage with each other *and* the books—centered on the classroom library—students' enthusiasm for reading and their interactions around books were hindered.

Lining up desks in rows enabled Colby's students to socially distance during the 2020–2021 school year, but it prevented them from having the proximity to one another that helps speed the development of a classroom reading community.

After winter break, Colby directed his attention to the classroom library and how kids were using it. Because social-distancing guidelines made it difficult for them to browse the collection together, Colby rearranged the books and their placement in the room. He created smaller sets of books for kids to browse. Because organic conversations about books were occurring less frequently, he gave more book talks and carved out more time for kids to give them, too.

> With an intentional focus on the classroom library, its design, purposes, and daily use, how could Colby inspire kids to read more, develop independent reading habits, and build reader-to-reader connections with each other?

Colby tinkered with the classroom library until the last few weeks of school. For example, when he noticed students were not reading many nonfiction books, he moved those books to a more conspicuous location three weeks before the end of the school year. It might seem pointless to make such a major change so close to summer break, but in Colby's mind whatever came of it would inform his decision-making for next year. Besides, if moving the books got a few more students reading nonfiction before the last day of school, that was a good thing.

It was a hard year, but Colby's beliefs about the importance of access to books, choice of books and writing topics, and frequent opportunities for kids to talk with each other about books were key in enticing his students to read more.

Colby spent part of the summer mulling over the previous school year and considering what he might tweak in response to students' learning needs and interests, particularly the classroom library. He could not stop thinking about it and how to change it. What worked? What didn't? What could be retooled, and what needed to be abandoned? Reflecting on students' use of the library and how the books were organized, he wondered how to leverage the collection to engage kids more than ever. What challenges did students have using the classroom library to find desirable books to read? What challenges did he have using it during conferences and instruction? With an intentional focus on the classroom library, its design, purposes, and daily use, how could Colby inspire kids to read more, develop independent reading habits, and build reader-to-reader connections with each other? What did Colby learn during the pandemic that will inform his work with students going forward? What role does the classroom library play?

And Another School Year Begins...

It's early July, and Donalyn is visiting Parma. The two of us weave around the furniture stacked in the unlit hallway to reach Colby's room at the end. The custodians have been deep cleaning the building and waxing the floors, so we tread only on the unwaxed tiles. We know better than to mess up the custodians' hard work! Parma Elementary doesn't have air conditioning, so we choose to work early in the day and leave the building before it gets too hot.

We've been chatting about Colby's classroom library all spring, but this is the first time we've been able to meet in person. The longer the two of us study literacy education and teach reading and writing, the more we recognize how much we still need to learn. We both share a willingness to reflect on what is working or not, and to remain open to what kids show us they need. After months of discussion, we had a rough idea of how to reenvision a classroom library. Our plan? Take Colby's classroom library apart and put it back together, so that it might work more effectively for him and his students.

For the next four days, we cleaned the library, weeded its books, and reorganized those that remained. We scrawled questions and notes on the whiteboards, made lists of books to replace, and exchanged a lot of family news and book recommendations. We talked and talked about the classroom library and how to maximize its potential, so that students would read more.

Donalyn and Colby piled weeded books throughout the classroom during their summer work in his classroom library.

This Book's Beginnings

This book began from those conversations. With an intentional focus on students' interactions within the classroom library, we wondered, how might the reading community and students' reading engagement grow?

Colby took whatever books he could get his hands on. He would sort through them and take promising ones to school. Over time, he had gathered a staggering number of books, which was not necessarily a good thing.

At that moment, we were standing between two school years and two groups of young readers—anticipating the incoming group's needs while trying to learn the last few lessons his former students taught us. The classroom library held a lot of the answers we sought. Every book seemingly reminded Colby of a kid who read it or a classroom experience tied to it. How could we streamline and leverage his classroom library to maximize his students' engagement with reading and positively influence their reading development? How could he periodically adjust the classroom library throughout the year in response to students' shifting needs and interests?

Moves We Made to Overhaul Colby's Classroom Library

We began by stripping the collection down to its most engaging books and reorganizing the space in response to the way kids used it. Do not get bogged down in the details of the moves that follow. Consider the reflective process behind our decision-making. What do you notice about your students' use of your classroom library? What daily challenges do you and your students experience? What would you change if you could?

Considered challenges to kids' access to books and reading behaviors because of how the library was organized.

Because the categories for the book bins were so broad, it was challenging for Colby and his students to find a specific book. For example, if there were 10 bins labeled Realistic Fiction T–Z, a child would have to dig through all of them before determining whether Kelly Yang's *Front Desk* was checked out or not. Series books were scattered throughout the alphabetical section by author.

The graphic novel section needed consolidating in one spot and reorganizing, which led us to making series and author/illustrator bins for many titles. Because the graphic novel section was popular and often congested, Colby had moved some of the graphic novel bins to other shelves around the classroom library. It was difficult for kids to find books, and they often wound up wandering around the room. Over time, authors and illustrators had continued a series or published more books, and many of them needed their own bins now so that they would be highlighted and easier for readers to identify and locate.

At the end of the year, as noted earlier, Colby relocated the nonfiction section to increase traffic and awareness after observing his students' reluctance to choose nonfiction texts for independent reading. He wanted to improve students' ability to browse and choose nonfiction to read.

The mountains of books made Colby realize that he needed to weed his classroom library throughout the school year and during the summer.

Weeded and cleaned the library.

Like many teachers, Colby took whatever books he could get his hands on. He would sort through them and take promising ones to school. Over time, he had gathered a staggering number of books, which was not necessarily a good thing. There were so many books wedged into the library that kids had to dig through lots of them when browsing. Some of the books that looked "promising" when Colby added them to the library were never read. Some were likely better suited to older or younger readers. Other books, once popular, were no longer relevant to his students. Quite a few of the nonfiction books he had acquired were outdated and unappealing. In general, there were many books that were worn or old.

We cleaned every bin and examined every book, ultimately removing approximately 25 percent of the collection. Books that were old, worn, damaged, or outdated were recycled. Books that were in good shape and reasonably current were added to the school's donation table.

Reorganized the lettering and labeling system for the bins.

The range for bins was too wide (A–K, L–S, and T–Z for all the fiction bins). There were multiple bins for each letter range—for example, there were 20 or more bins labeled "L–S." Kids could browse, but they could not find a specific book they wanted without looking through lots of bins. The range of bins needed to be narrower (A–B, C–D, and so on). Now when looking for a particular book, Colby and the kids would have fewer bins to search.

Popular authors and series, which were spread across several bins, needed to be consolidated in fewer bins for ease of sharing and locating.

Made a list of high-demand books and replacements for popular titles.

As we sorted through books and reunited many series books with their siblings, the two of us kept a running list of the books that were missing from series runs. A series that lacks a few titles is unlikely to engage readers for long. The two of us have often invested in multiple copies of the first book or two in popular series, so that kids can read them even if one copy is lost.

When we came across a book that was too damaged or old to keep, Colby determined whether it still had kid appeal or value. If so, it was added to the replacement list, too. Many old and damaged books were removed from the collection and not replaced because they were no longer relevant or current for students.

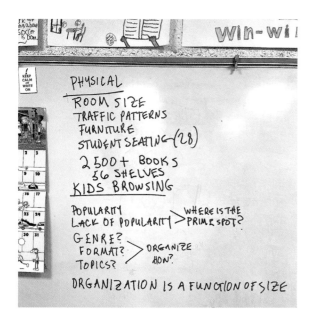

Researched new books and solicited recommendations.

If you put two readers in the same room together for four days, they will share a truckload of book recommendations! For every book we put our hands on, we could connect it to another book we loved by the same author or on a similar topic.

Discovering gaps in the collection took us onto the Internet to track down titles that would meet particular needs. Evaluating,

As Donalyn and Colby worked in the classroom library, they kept track of their thinking on the whiteboard.

sorting, and discussing every book in the classroom library led us to suggest many other books kids might read and add more books to Colby's wish list. While these steps only scratched the surface of the effort Colby would invest into curating the classroom library with students in mind, this deep weed and clean is a beneficial process for winnowing down your classroom library to its most effective and useful materials.

If we taught at the same school, we would evaluate Donalyn's classroom library next. It helps to have other perspectives about your classroom library. What biases and gaps within the collection might emerge? What can a colleague see about the traffic flow or organization that you might not? What challenges do you see? Bouncing ideas off a colleague who also has a classroom library might help you work through solutions to those challenges. There are many suggestions for weeding your classroom library throughout this book.

About This Book

With this book, consider us your colleagues down the hall. We share our processes for evaluating the library, resources we use, and practical strategies we have developed over the years for managing a collection and using the books to engage readers.

In Chapter 1, we contextualize classroom libraries by making clear that they should be just one source of books for students, along with the school, home, and public library. Students need many access streams to become passionate, proficient readers. In Chapter 2, we explain how to build your collection and organize your space by focusing on key considerations: quantity, diversity, currency and relevance, and organization and use. In Chapters 3 and 4, we look at Colby's classroom library across a school year, from the very beginning, when he introduces the library to students, to the very end, when he sets the stage for summer reading.

While our experiences are valid and valuable, they do not represent every perspective or community, so we have invited several experienced educators from a range of backgrounds to share their ideas and advice. They offer "commonsense suggestions" for examining students' book-access needs and fine-tuning your classroom library to entice and challenge your students to read more and to read more joyfully.

We hope this book provides you with tools to look at your library through a different lens, curate it with students in mind, and tap its full potential throughout the year.

—Donalyn Miller and Colby Sharp, Spring 2022

CHAPTER ONE

Giving Kids Books in the Classroom— and Beyond

While this is a book about classroom libraries, your students' book access cannot begin and end in your room. To create a classroom library that effectively meets your students' reading needs and interests, you must consider their book access—both at school and home—all year long. A classroom library supplements other sources of books; it is not supposed to provide students with all of their reading material.

Putting Classroom Libraries in Context

How does access to books support your students' literacy development? Where do classroom libraries fit in? Let's take a look at book access throughout children's lives—from access to the public library, the home library, the school library, and—yes—the classroom library. Classroom libraries are not year-round or all-day sources of books. They supplement the school library and community resources, which serve a broader range of patrons.

Educators and caregivers often wonder, "How many books do kids need for them to have meaningful access?" There is no simple answer because so much depends on the quality of the books, the sources of books in your community, and the abilities and interests of the readers. Kids need to read widely—they need to read all sorts of texts on all sorts of topics and experiences. They need to read voluminously—they need to develop good reading habits. Without continuous access to reading material, they struggle to find books to read and build those habits. For decades, studies have shown a connection between the volume and variety of students' reading experiences, and their mastery of age-appropriate reading milestones (NAEP, 2015; Harvey et. al, 2021).

Kids need to read widely—they need to read all sorts of texts on all sorts of topics and experiences. They need to read voluminously—they need to develop good reading habits.

Furthermore, researchers have determined that increasing students' book access influences their academic and personal success (Neuman & Celano, 2012; Kim & Quinn, 2013; Constantino, 2014). Young people need a book flood—continuous access to a wide variety of engaging and relevant texts. When they have it, they are more likely to take advantage of opportunities to read and spend more time reading (Neuman & Knapczyk, 2018). Drawing from 70,000 case studies across 27 countries, sociologists found that access to books influences students' education levels as much as growing up with college-educated parents and caregivers (Evans et. al, 2010).

Despite the extensive evidence that book access matters, too many children live in book "deserts." They don't have access to current, interesting books that represent themselves and others (Neuman & Moland, 2016; Wong 2016). Many brick-and-mortar bookstores have closed. Public libraries have reduced their hours and services. School districts have cut library positions and slashed funding for reading materials and patron outreach. Some administrators have instituted restrictive book-selection policies or reading management programs that reduce students' access to books even more. Few schools provide adequate funding for trade books in language arts classrooms. According to a survey of thousands of teachers and librarians, most classroom teachers self-fund their classroom libraries and a significant number of librarians do the same for the school (Miller & Sharp, 2018).

Families need more support and resources for increasing books in the home and acquiring library cards. Examining children's access to reading material in two Philadelphia communities—one middle-class and one low-income neighborhood—Neuman and Celano concluded that the lack of access to print in low-income communities had a long-lasting effect on children's literacy development (2012). Black children, children in poverty, and Indigenous children—especially in urban and rural areas—are more likely to live in book deserts because they don't have the school and community resources to provide regular access to text. Public libraries were most effective in addressing the disparities in book access in the communities Neuman and Celano studied because they were the most recognizable and accessible sources of books and reading materials. While your school library and classroom library offer significant book outlets for students during the school year, the most stable and consistent sources of reading materials all year are their community public libraries and home libraries, which we address next.

Public Libraries

Public libraries provide the most equitable access to reading materials for the communities they serve. For many people, it is hard to understand why kids need more sources of books—including classroom libraries—when the public library is right down the road. We have heard every counter-argument to funding all sources that you can imagine: "Isn't the public library enough? Why do kids need more books?" "If kids need books, their parents can take them to the library—problem solved." This privileged stance toward public library access presumes that when students tell us they do not go to the library, it is because of some flaw in their parents. Parents must underestimate the importance of reading, or libraries. However, for many families, access to the library involves logistical, social, or financial barriers, versus a motivational one.

Parents and caregivers tell us that they do not use the public library for many reasons: they have a conflict, such as work, during library hours; they lack transportation; they cannot meet the residency requirements to get a library card (such as providing a utility bill); or they avoid interacting with government agencies because of their residency status or suspicions related to their status. For young people, some libraries ban unaccompanied minors to prevent "loitering" or issue policies that discourage teens from gathering in the library.

Families tell us that the threat of fines and fees makes them think twice about borrowing library materials. Some don't sign up for library cards in the first place because they fear racking up fines. A Texas law defines the failure to return library materials as theft, and it can result in heavy fines and possible jail time in some municipalities!

In response to the declining use of libraries and changing needs of patrons, many public library systems have loosened their fine and fee policies. The New York Public Library, Chicago Public Library, Dallas Public Library, and many other city, suburban, and rural libraries have done away with them entirely. According to Sarah Vantrease, public services divisions manager for the Sonoma County Library, "Research shows that charging fines doesn't make a difference in whether people bring back books on time. Instead, we see that fines drive people away." In communities where the public libraries charge fines, fewer people use the library. Because public libraries are the main source of books for kids, fine and fee programs hurt those who rely on them for books. If you are interested in learning more about the national wave to change those programs, visit the Urban Library Council's Fine Free Map online.

School and classroom libraries provide students with reading materials during the school year, but for continuous access, 365 days a year, reading materials must also be available in the community.

As the school year winds down, the Jackson County Public Library brings its bookmobile to Colby's school so his fifth graders and other students can check out books and sign up for library cards. This is an important service because many kids don't visit the public library consistently.

COLBY'S CLASSROOM

Connecting Students With the Public Library

As we inch closer to the end of the school year, one thing I stress out about the most is what will happen to my students when they say goodbye to our reading community and classroom library? What will happen to their reading lives when they are no longer spending seven hours a day with their classmates? Will they be able to find a reading community outside of school? What will happen to their book access? Will they carve out time to read without the structure of the school day?

The public library could be the answer to many of those questions, but I've noticed over the years that fewer and fewer of my fifth graders regularly visit their public library. In the fall, I asked my kids how many of them had been to the public library in the last year, and only one hand went up.

To motivate them, I tell them about my weekly visits to our public library, which is located a few blocks from our school. When I'm conferring with them, I have the public library tab open on my computer, so that we can put holds on books the kids want to read that aren't in our classroom or school library. When those books show up in our classroom a few days later, the kids are astonished by how easy it is for me to get just about any book in less than a week.

The more I talk about the public library and bring in library books for them to read, the more my kids start using the public library. Recently, Wyatt told the class about how he and his mom went to the library branch near the grocery store and checked out the latest books in the Dragon Masters series. During spring break, Ava went to our local branch with her parents and brother and got her own library card. She used the card to check out a bunch of books to read.

In mid-April the Jackson District Library's bookmobile came to our school—and it was a magical experience. It was filled from floor to ceiling with books. My kids were literally jumping up and down as they browsed the shelves. Before the bookmobile's visit, only four of my students had library cards. By the end of the visit, all 27 of them had one! And most of them checked out public-library books for the first time.

When we returned to class, we talked about the power of the library card. My students were excited to learn they could put holds on books and use interlibrary loan to check out just about any book that they wanted. They were also excited to learn they could check out ebooks and audiobooks, which they could read and listen to on their school-issued iPads. I told them that we would be exploring the online features that their new library card provided over the next few weeks.

In the coming weeks, we will walk from school to our local library, with our library cards in hand. Kids will meet our librarians, browse shelves, and learn about summer reading programs. My hope is that visiting the public library and signing kids up for library cards will help them step toward independence.

The public library offers a relatively stable community source of reading materials, but the most personal library is the one that students have at home. Working to provide all students with at least a few books of their own can support their reading development and growing independence—and, hopefully, inspire them to become lifelong public-library patrons.

Home Libraries

When school is the primary source of books for kids, their access to books depends on their access to school. When the pandemic shuttered many schools in the spring of 2020, many children lost their book access overnight. While many schools addressed the problem by distributing books, devices, assistive technology, and reading databases to students, it took time.

Community access to books dried up, too. Many public libraries closed, and librarians redesigned their book-loaning programs and processes to comply with federal safety guidelines for handling materials. Without access to the public library, many families lost access to the Internet, as well as print materials. As a result, some kids could not keep reading. This begs the question: How can we ensure more equitable book access, even when libraries and schools close?

When kids own books at home, they read more and show more interest in reading. Clark and Poulton surveyed more than 18,000 school-age children and found that those who had access to many books at home spent more time reading, showed higher reading engagement, read more widely, and finished more books (2010).

In a meta-analysis of 108 studies evaluating programs that lend or donate books, researchers at Reading Is Fundamental (RIF) found that giving kids access to print materials is associated with positive behavioral, educational, and emotional outcomes (2010). Access to print materials:

- improves children's reading performance.
- is instrumental in helping children learn the basics of reading.
- causes children to read more and for longer lengths of time.
- produces improved attitudes toward reading and learning among children.

While the two of us advocate for more school library and classroom funding for reading materials, we encourage community organizations to invest in reading materials in children's homes. We also encourage investment in technology support and assistance to access reading materials in formats other than print. According to NEA's landmark 2007 study, To Read or Not to Read, avid adult readers in the United States reached higher levels of educational attainment, volunteered more in their communities, and voted more often. Society benefits when more people read.

> Beyond its positive impact on literacy development and academic growth, book ownership strengthens children's identities as readers.

Home libraries provide individualized book access based on children's interests and the topics and stories their families value. Beyond its positive impact on literacy development and academic growth, book ownership strengthens children's identities as readers. Kids are more likely to see themselves as readers and engage in literary conversations when they grow up with books (Muhammad, 2020).

How can we guarantee that all kids in our communities own at least a few books? We recommend looking beyond the school and partnering with community groups and the public library to create book donation and distribution programs. Look for donors through local businesses and organizations. Talk with parents and caregivers about the importance of books in the home, and offer resources for finding affordable, relevant books. We suggest some sources of low-cost and free books on page 36.

Providing Access to Technology for Reading

It might seem like everyone has a smartphone these days—even our youngest students—but it is not true. The switch to online learning has underscored the unequal access to technology for many children. According to the Pew Research Foundation, 25 percent of households in the United States lack consistent broadband

Internet access. Fifteen percent of U.S. adults depend on a smartphone for their Internet access. Even when families own a device for their children to use, such as a tablet or desktop computer, it is difficult to provide access to that device when several children need it at the same time. Work with families to identify and solve technology needs that might impede students' ability to read at home, and offer training and materials as necessary. Some schools and public libraries will provide patrons and their children with devices, hotspots, and assistive technology such as text-to-voice programs to support schoolwork and reading at home.

School Libraries and Librarians

Increasing students' book ownership and helping families acquire library cards are the two best ways to ensure that kids have access to reading material 365 days a year. Another way is to make sure kids are taking full advantage of the school library—the literacy hub for everyone in the building. The school library offers the most consistent source of books and technology for many kids. With a sizable program and book budget, a professional school librarian develops the collection, provides teachers with curriculum support and resources, and makes kids aware of books and authors.

Unfortunately, many schools do not have a centralized library, and even when they do, they may not have a credentialed librarian on staff. Examining data from 13,000 school districts during the 2018–2019 school year, researchers found that (Lance & Kachel, 2021):

- Three out of 10 districts had no librarians in any of their schools.
- More than 4.4 million students in high-poverty (50 percent+) districts had no librarians.
- Almost 3.1 million students in predominantly Hispanic districts were without school librarians.

- Almost 4.8 million students in predominantly non-white districts were without school librarians.
- Smaller and rural districts were more likely to have no librarians than larger and suburban districts.
- Nine out of 10 charter schools had no school librarians.

Cutting school librarians seems shortsighted for administrators driven to increase students' scores on standardized assessments. For decades, researcher Keith Curry Lance and his colleagues have studied the effectiveness of school librarians in the United States, including their effect on test scores. Their findings show that the size of the library program—determined by the size of the staff and collection—is the best school-based predictor of academic achievement. The instructional role of the librarian influences the collection, which influences every child and adult in the building (Lance & Hofschire, 2012). When librarians are cut, test scores fall. Students from low-income households, emergent bilingual students (who are still developing their language skills in English), and bilingual students are affected most. But, not surprisingly, all students' book access drops precipitously. School districts have lost librarians even as student populations grew 7 percent across the United States (Lance & Kachel, 2021). Eliminating librarians, as well as qualified support staff, will continue until funding them becomes a priority (Lance & Kachel, 2018).

And even when the library is staffed, the people in charge may lack any training in librarianship or professional credentials. They may be paraprofessionals or school volunteers. Their job may be limited to shelving books, managing circulation, and addressing technology needs. Without professional training in developing collections and matching readers with books, any person would find it challenging to curate a high-quality collection, help teachers and students to locate and evaluate materials, and engage readers.

> When librarians are cut, test scores fall.

Even when schools have trained librarians, the library often may not be available to kids because, for example, it may be closed for many days for meetings and testing. Librarians may be pulled from the library for other duties or reassigned to cover classrooms. District or campus policies may determine when the library opens for the school year and when it closes for the summer. In some cases, the library may not open for several weeks or may close weeks early because of inventory or database needs. In such instances, the school library is not accessible for students to browse, find, and check out books. Administrators concerned about students' literacy development must put school library funding and staffing first because the library serves the whole school population.

Advocating for School Librarians and Libraries

If adults do not advocate for school libraries and librarians, kids will continue to lose. Explore and share the following resources when talking with district leaders and community members about why kids need libraries and qualified librarians.

- Scholastic's *School Libraries Work!* (Terry & Lance, 2016) is a downloadable brief that summarizes the current research around the effectiveness of school libraries and librarians.
- The *School Library Journal* article "Fighting Cuts: How to Keep Librarians in Schools" (Yorio, 2018) includes practical suggestions and extensive resources for schools and districts facing looming library cuts.
- The American Library Association's *Frontline Advocacy for School Libraries Toolkit* contains abundant suggestions and resources for promoting your library program.
- The nonprofit library advocacy organization Every Library (everylibrary.org) works with federal, state, and local legislatures to protect and fund public and school library programs.

Classroom Libraries

Like many of you, we worked for years to build our classroom libraries because we have seen how providing access to books, along with guidance and encouragement in choosing books, has helped our students grow as readers. Classroom libraries are so much more than random books on shelves. How can classroom libraries support students?

Increasing Access With Classroom Libraries

In addition to having access to public, home, and school libraries, children and adolescents benefit from meaningful access to books and other texts in their classrooms. Robust, curated classroom libraries substantially improve students' daily interactions with books and give you the ability to offer recommendations for independent reading and quickly find materials to meet your instructional needs.

Students in classrooms with robust, curated libraries have more positive attitudes about reading, interact more with books, spend more time reading, and show higher reading achievement (NAEP, 2005). By increasing students' reading motivation and widening their reading experiences, classroom libraries support the development of reading skills and positive reading identities. According to the National Council of Teachers of English (2017), classroom libraries:

- motivate students by encouraging voluntary and recreational reading.
- help them develop an extensive array of literacy strategies and skills.
- provide access to a wide range of reading materials that reflect students' abilities and interests.
- enhance opportunities for both assigned and casual reading.
- provide choice in reading materials for self-engagement.
- strengthen and encourage authentic literate exchanges among young people and adolescents.
- provide access to digitized reading materials that may help to foster the development of technological literacy skills.
- validate and promote the acceptance and inclusion of students' diverse identities and experiences.
- create opportunities to cultivate an informed citizenry.

As elementary and middle school teachers, we have seen firsthand how classroom libraries contribute to strengthening students' reading and influencing their motivation and enthusiasm for reading. That said, a classroom library cannot replace a school library that is managed by a professional librarian and contains an extensive collection. The school library serves all the readers in the school. The classroom library serves a specific group of students. In many schools and districts, shortsighted initiatives that cannibalize school library budgets to fund classroom libraries have dramatically reduced students' access to books and qualified librarians. Yes, this is a book about classroom libraries, and we are strong advocates for them. But supporting classroom libraries at the expense of a school library led by a professional librarian, does not improve outcomes for kids.

> If you are launching a classroom library initiative, involve your school librarians deeply in the process.

If you are launching a classroom library initiative, involve your school librarians deeply in the process. After all, your librarian is likely one of the only people in your school with training and experience in curating book collections and following trends in children's and young adult literature. Ask your librarian for resources and advice when selecting books and materials for your classroom library. Collaborative efforts between librarians and teachers increase students' book access more consistently.

In some schools, librarians fear (or even resent) classroom library initiatives. They feel their education and experience are not valued when collections are built without their input. Librarian educator Jennifer LaGarde explains from where this fear stems and describes the potential of classroom libraries when teachers and librarians work together to build collections.

Increasing Book Access Across the School
Jennifer LaGarde

Librarians and Classroom Libraries

Donalyn: In *Game Changer! Book Access for All Kids* (Miller & Sharp, 2018), you did a great job of addressing the territoriality that many librarians feel for the word "library," and their mistrust of "classroom libraries" and their perceived value. You have helped me personally understand why such nuances in word choices are a big deal to librarians. They are losing their jobs. There are shortsighted (or uniformed) administrators who don't understand that cutting librarians and siphoning funding from the school library for classroom libraries are not okay.

Jennifer: There are school districts where there's no historical memory of what a school librarian does because there have not been school librarians in their schools or districts for many years. There are some librarians—every single year—spending a large portion of their professional lives fighting to prove that they deserve to exist. When you're in fight-or-flight mode, you let emotions drive your reactions. This negative response to classroom libraries—it's driven out of fear.

Teachers and librarians—we all want kids to have more access to books. Adults must understand how library collections of all stripes really democratize school for kids who don't have resources at home. It's a no-brainer that adults would want schools to have classroom libraries and centralized school libraries. We want administrators to have libraries. We want bookshelves in the cafeteria! This reality is hard to see when you are living in fear of losing your job.

Colby: I've been in this district since 1986 (as a student and now a teacher). I don't remember—at least at the elementary level—having a librarian. I've never attended a school with a librarian or taught in a school with one.

Jennifer: I went to many schools without libraries....

Donalyn: Teachers and librarians are forced to squabble over a finite pool of resources, which often has more to do with priority setting than it does with funding. One administrator who doesn't understand the value of school libraries and librarians could halt or limit information and resource access for every kid in the school. Even when administrators recognize the importance of library programs and staffing, they may be driven to make tough choices, such as adding a special education teacher or reducing class sizes by adding another general education teacher.

Jennifer: The average tenure of a principal in most districts is really only a few years. The revolving door of leadership in which every person has a different priority, and a different agenda makes it very difficult for districts to formatively assess their practices and make some changes based on the results.

Donalyn: If you don't have school and district leaders who consistently communicate that school librarians and libraries are important and kids need books in the classroom, then those resources might not be sustained. Leadership for such initiative cannot become personnel dependent on a few people.

Advocating for Your Classroom Library

Donalyn: What advice would you give English teachers who want to advocate for their classroom library? How can they show administrators, parents, or even the school librarian why kids benefit from a classroom library? What should they say?

Jennifer: One of the reasons that I switched careers from classroom teacher to librarian is because libraries are one of the last remaining egalitarian institutions or concepts in the world. Libraries provide equitable access to every person—regardless of the color of their skin, how much money they make, what they believe, who they love—all of it. And classroom libraries are no exception. They may operate with different tools, but classroom libraries are a tool for the classroom teacher to democratize resources for students.

When I talk to my own preservice librarian students about how to design their public and school libraries—or help teachers in creating their classroom libraries—I have them consider the kids who have the most needs. These might include kids who are living in poverty, are experiencing some kind of trauma, or have learning or social-emotional needs, and so on.

In your school, you decide what those needs are. The other half of the Venn diagram are the kids who participate the least in school. They might be kids who have attendance problems, put their heads down during class, or don't participate in any extracurricular activities. Where those two groups overlap—that's the kids you build your library for—the kids with the most needs and the lowest school participation. The library's purpose is to make resources equitable. So, when advocating for classroom libraries, I would focus on how this access increases equity. It's not about reading scores. It's about putting a practical strategy in front of equity initiatives that sometimes exist in name only. Administrators can direct money into equity work and can see some measurable results. Classroom and school library data can show the effectiveness of such initiatives.

Good libraries of all kinds are really about creating a better world, because they give all people access to the resources they need. That's why kids need classroom libraries and school libraries—to increase the likelihood that the ones who really need access are going to get it.

Donalyn: A school library, of course, provides that function for all the children in the school. But kids benefit from the fingertip, on-demand access that a classroom library provides, too.

Jennifer: Regardless of how accessible you think the school library is, or how wonderful of a librarian you are, there are some kids who may not feel comfortable coming to the library or talking with you. But they have a really good relationship with their teacher. Why wouldn't you want to work in concert to create collections throughout the school that fit together like puzzle pieces?

Young people need access to a wide variety of books and other reading materials to become proficient readers and develop positive reading identities. Increasing students' book access through classroom libraries is just one more way to give kids access to books on a consistent basis. In the next chapter, we will consider how to build a streamlined, relevant, and engaging collection that is responsive to your students' needs and interests.

TIME TO REFLECT

- **How have you experienced book floods and book deserts in your life?** As a young person, did you own books or have regular access to them? How do you access books now? How has your access changed over your lifetime?

- **What about your students?** How does access to books vary among them? What sources for reading material do they have beyond your classroom? Your school?

- **What resources does your public library offer?** What are the requirements for acquiring a library card and borrowing materials? What are the fine and fee policies? What barriers do you see to public library use?

CHAPTER TWO

Building the Collection and Organizing the Library Space

Like most of you, the two of us have been scrounging for books our entire teaching careers. We have bought books at garage sales and used bookstores, collected advance copies and discount copies at conferences, accepted book donations from families, rescued castoffs from other teachers or librarians, used any possible classroom funds to buy books, and cannibalized our children's home libraries as they outgrew them so we could take books from them to school. While those piecemeal methods for finding books helped us fill our classroom library shelves, they did not allow us to add many new books to our collection or intentionally curate it.

Building a collection is about much more than putting books on the shelves. It takes purposeful, knowledgeable effort. You will never finish creating a classroom library, because every year brings different kids and different books. For every enduring favorite type of book you keep in your library, such as penguin books, there are just as many that have their season and fade away, such as slime-making books. (Please tell us the slime craze is over!) No catalog offers a magic classroom library set that will meet all your students' reading interests and needs. One size does not fit all.

Classroom Library Considerations

When setting out to create a classroom library or reimagine your existing one, where should you start? The two of us consider four components:

1 **Quantity:** How many students will use the collection? What is the student-to-book ratio? What access do students have to books elsewhere?

2 **Diversity:** How broad and inclusive is your classroom library? Does it contain a wide range of reading levels, genres, topics, and formats? Do the books accurately represent a variety of racial, ethnic, and social backgrounds, lived experiences, and perspectives? Are the books free of harmful stereotypes and biases?

3 **Currency and Relevance:** How up-to-date is the collection? Are the nonfiction books outdated or inaccurate? Do some of the books match students' personal interests, such as hobbies, crafts, sports, and popular culture? Does your collection include texts that align with curricula for content areas such as social studies and science?

4 **Organization and Use:** Is the library space inviting and accessible to all your students? Is there enough space for all the books? Can more than one student use the library at a time? Can students successfully locate books without your support? Do you have a user-friendly checkout and return system in place (if you want one)?

Let's look at each of those components and see how, together, they provide a strong foundation for your classroom library.

1. Quantity

How many books do you need in your classroom library? When we ask most teachers that question, they reply, "More, that's how many books we need. More." Few teachers will turn down books because they know kids must read lots of them. Teachers need books for instructional purposes, too. Expert advice on the ideal number of books varies widely—anywhere from 1,000 (Allington, 2013) to a ratio based on books per student (Reutzel & Fawson, 2002). To determine how many books you need to support your students, consider the following factors.

Access Points Within the School

- Where can students find books outside your classroom?
- Do you have a school library?
- How often do students go to the library to choose books?
- What are the library's operating hours? How often is it open to students?

Access Points Beyond the School

- Where can students locate and acquire books outside of school?
- Do you have an accessible public library with an adequate children's and young-adult literature collection?
- Do students have library cards?
- Where can students purchase new or used books in your community?
- What is the quality and price of books at those outlets?

A well-curated school library is the most dependable source of reading materials for students. If your school does not have a library—or it does, but it is often closed or has policies that discourage use (such as fines for overdue books)—your classroom library can fill your students' access gap with a good assortment of books.

Students spend most of their lives away from school, but they need access to books 365 days a year. As we discussed in Chapter One, no matter how much effort your school puts into improving students' book access, the best free source of reading materials is your local public library. When more resources are available, book ownership supports students' personal reading identities and provides the most stable access. Working to ensure that all students have library cards and own at least a few books of their own goes a long way to providing wraparound access.

Administrative Support

- Does your school provide books or funding for school and classroom libraries?
- Does your school have a librarian?
- Is the school library adequately funded?
- Is there administrative support for independent reading at your school?

Without backing from school leaders, it is difficult to build and maintain a collection or use it effectively with kids. But when those leaders provide funding for school libraries, librarians, and classroom libraries, and communicate the importance of book access to students' literacy development, teachers are more likely to maintain collections, refresh them, and increase the number of books they contain (Vu, 2021).

Patrons

- How many students wander through your classroom every day?
- Who borrows books?
- Do you often loan books to students' siblings and other family members?
- What about former students or students from other classrooms?

If you have 100 students or more, you will need more books than a teacher with a self-contained classroom of 24 students. If you are free with your book lending and the classroom library provides reading materials for more than a single class of students, you will need to have more books. When students in other classes or colleagues frequently borrow books, consider how those loans reduce the number of books on hand.

Instructional Needs

- How will you use the books with students?
- Is the collection solely for independent reading?
- Are you using it for inquiry projects or other learning activities?
- Do you need multiple copies of the same book for partner reads or book clubs?

If students require more than one copy for various assignments, you may need more titles to meet their needs. Your ability to use your classroom library for instructional purposes is limited when it doesn't contain enough books to offer students a lot of variety or choices.

There is no magic number of books you should have—or formula for determining that number. The best classroom libraries are built with students in mind. Considering how your classroom library fits into a larger network of students' book sources is the best guide for determining how many books you need.

There is no magic number of books you should have—or formula for determining that number. The best classroom libraries are built with students in mind.

Where to Find More Books and Funding

When we were writing *Game Changer! Book Access for All Kids*, we surveyed thousands of U.S. and Canadian teachers and librarians in public, private, and charter schools about funding for books. Eighty-three percent of teachers told us that they received zero to 25 percent of the funding for their classroom libraries from their schools or districts (Miller & Sharp, 2018). A significant number of librarians told us they were financially subsidizing the school library! The schools that dedicate significant funding to prep materials and tutoring for standardized testing dedicate little funding to the one resource proven time and again to increase students' test scores across the board: books (Krashen, 2013)!

When schools rely on teachers to purchase books for their own classrooms, it becomes an equity issue. Book access for kids should not depend on their teacher's willingness, ability, and/or finances to provide the books. Teacher and author Penny Kittle launched the Book Love Foundation in direct response to the needs of the high school teachers she spoke with during her workshops. She explained her impetus to start the grant program during our interview for this book: "Every high school teacher I ran into felt like they were alone in this work of engaging kids with independent reading. They were alone in providing choice. They were alone in building a classroom library and had no support. The high school English department budget always went to core texts. That struck me. The people I was encouraging to promote independent reading had no access to funding for books. The mission from the start is that teachers need books that kids want to read if they are going to be able to shift the narrative about reading."

We must continue to advocate for librarians and teachers to receive funding for books and other reading materials. This is a systemic concern. We also recognize that you need funding now! Here are a few ideas and resources to get you started.

Sources for Book Grants

The Book Love Foundation
Teacher and author Penny Kittle began the Book Love Foundation, which awards grants to elementary and secondary teachers for classroom libraries. The foundation hosts an annual summer book club for teachers that offers low-cost opportunities to build your book knowledge and connect with like-minded educators and authors.

The Snapdragon Book Foundation
The Snapdragon Grant was created by a Texas librarian who wanted to increase children's book access. The grant funds magazine subscriptions and books for school libraries and classrooms.

Dollar General Literacy Foundation Grant Programs
Discount store chain Dollar General offers grants for community literacy programs, including adult literacy and summer reading.

You can find all of these sources for book grants online.

First Book Founded in 1992 as an effort to reduce book deserts, First Book provides free books to Title I schools through its Book Bank and sells new books at a significant discount through its First Book Marketplace.

Open eBooks For qualifying Title I schools, this federal program provides access to thousands of ebooks.

Reading Is Fundamental RIF is one of the most successful and enduring book-donation programs in the United States.

Public Library Your local library most likely offers materials such as ebooks and audiobooks that students can access for free at home.

You can find these sources for low-cost or free books online.

Create a shared document (such as a Google Sheet) for school staff to record grant opportunities and local sources for funding, such as community organizations and literacy programs. Ask your Better Business Bureau or Chamber of Commerce about grants or discounts from local businesses. Investigate programs through local universities and colleges. Check with your professional organizations, too. Ask your school PTA/PTO leadership if they can support classroom libraries. While funding sources change often, we list a few well-regarded, longstanding ones on page 35.

Talk with your school librarian about checking out text sets for book clubs, supplemental reading for curricular units and genre studies, and so on. These rotating collections keep your selections fresh, extend your classroom resources, and reinforce the connection between the school library and the daily work of the classroom. Adding books to the classroom library excites kids and creates opportunities for previewing, sharing, and talking about books they might read.

2. Diversity

Reading widely not only increases students' reading achievement, it can also keep readers engaged. Books have always opened up the world for kids. When we cannot travel with our feet, we can travel within the pages of a book. Kids need access to books that reflect their own experiences and points of view, as well as those that reflect the experiences and points of view of others to expand their understanding (Derman-Sparks, 2013). The books we promote through displays, lists, and book talks; the books we read aloud and use for mini-lessons; and the books we shelve in the classroom and school library have the potential to engage children with the whole world and its people.

Social and Cultural Representation

What are the books you currently share with students, as well as the class conversations around those books, communicating? Whose voices and experiences are valued? Whose voices are missing? The books we offer through our classroom libraries should expand our students' world, not narrow it.

The lack of equitable representation in curriculum and library collections has been a lasting problem in many communities. Because of the systemic grip of white supremacy, many schools' reading lists, textbooks, library collections, and classroom resources fail to depict accurately or equitably the wide-ranging stories and voices of our human experience. This erasure, stereotyping, or marginalizing of entire cultures, ethnicities, nationalities, religions, genders, and sexual orientations denies children and teens access to accurate information and stories. When historically marginalized kids cannot see themselves, their families, or their communities reflected in the texts and media we read and view at school, educators reinforce prejudices and biases and push our most vulnerable kids into the margins—further oppressing them (Naidoo, 2014).

Many children and adolescents lack access to books and other media portraying historically marginalized groups and people, including their own families and communities. From an identity standpoint, what does it communicate to kids when their school and the adults running it ignore or reject their existence through their book choices? How engaged are kids going to be with reading when they never find books that relate to their experiences? No, readers do not need to connect personally with every book. However, there is no shortage of books in schools that reflect the experiences of white, Christian, straight people. If our goal is to include more kids in the reading experience, the books we offer them must be more inclusive and relevant.

While many white educators have made efforts in recent years to diversify their collections and become more knowledgeable about books, conversations about the need for accurate representation are not new or trendy. Educators and families from underrepresented groups have questioned and challenged bigoted or absent portrayals of their families and communities in children's books for a long time (Larrick, 1965; Makarechi, 2015).

As Dr. Rudine Sims Bishop beautifully captured in her oft-quoted vision, young people need mirrors that reflect their own experiences, windows that offer a glimpse into the lives of people with different experiences, and sliding-glass doors that connect us to our imaginations and the broader world (1990). The media, including books, that young people read, view, and listen to, has a powerful influence on how they see themselves, their personal identity development, and how they see others (Tatum, 2009; Ahmed, 2018; Muhammad, 2020).

A library collection must reflect not only the stories and histories of our students and their families, but also the stories and histories of others, all year long—not just during certain months or holidays.

In our work in schools, we have seen books placed in separate baskets labeled "diverse"—"othering" those books by setting them apart from the real collection. Well-meaning teachers and librarians, in an effort to make books more conspicuous, may be unwittingly preventing kids from checking them out by communicating that there is something about them—and the people portrayed in them—that does not belong. A library collection must reflect not only the stories and histories of our students and their families, but also the stories and histories of others, all year long—not just during certain months or holidays. Additionally, the books teachers and librarians read, share, and promote should capture a range of stories and experiences, not just those of suffering and trauma. As scholar and school administrator Chad Everett wrote (2017), "All readers should be able to find texts that affirm their lives and experiences. All readers should be able to find texts that affirm the lives and experiences of others."

Of course, it will take more to dismantle institutional and social bigotry than diversifying our classroom libraries. However, we know that books have the power to change hearts and minds. As white educators, we know that our efforts to improve and increase the variety of books in our classroom libraries and instruction have directly influenced our personal educations about the world we live in and the experiences of people beyond our communities. Books give kids a place to expand their horizons when geography does not.

When evaluating books that feature stories and experiences that differ from yours, it can be difficult to determine whether they capture accurate and affirming representations. Rely on scholars in the field and respected review sources. Follow publishers' YouTube and social media accounts and watch new release previews and interviews with authors and illustrators. Search for reviews from people who share the same culture or lived experiences as the characters and people in the books. Interact with other teachers and librarians online and seek out connections with educators from a variety of cultures, nationalities, backgrounds, regions, and job assignments.

We have listed a few resources and tools to get you started. Follow the creators of these resources, and you will find more.

Resources for Finding and Evaluating Children's and Young Adult Literature

- **We Need Diverse Books**
- **The Brown Bookshelf**
- **American Indians in Children's Literature**
- **Guide for Selecting Anti-Bias Books**
- **The Anti-Defamation League's Assessing Children's Literature**

Search for these resources by name for more information.

As many teachers and librarians across North America strive to diversify their book collections and offer students more accurate, current, and inclusive texts to read, some bigoted people are actively resisting their schools' and libraries' efforts to provide more representation in the collection. Incidents of book banning and book challenges are at an all-time high. In some cases, book-banning groups use book lists meant to promote diverse literature as lists of books to target for challenges (Harris & Alter, 2022).

Censorship and Book Challenges Reduce Access

As we discussed in Chapter One, access to books begins with ensuring that students can get reading materials and the technology required to read them. But true access includes children and teens' social and cultural access to the stories of our world and its people and open access to the intellectual knowledge of human thought. In too many schools purporting to offer students choices in reading materials, collections have been restricted because of book challenges from outraged and organized parents. Under the guise of "protecting" children from obscenity and radical ideas, censorship stems from bigotry and fear. Skim the annual Banned Book Lists compiled by the American Library Association, and it does not take long to see that most of the books banned in libraries across the United States feature the stories and experiences of marginalized people—particularly Black people, Indigenous people, and people of color (BIPOC) and LGBTQ+ people.

Soft Censorship Is Insidious

Censorship affects book access in ways that can be invisible to many readers. While we have all seen dramatic images of book burnings and heated school board meetings, most censorship in schools is more insidious. One of our mentors, Dr. Teri S. Lesesne, often spoke out against "soft censorship," or the refusal to add books to the collection because an administrator, librarian, or teacher fears *potential* reprisal (Miller & Lesesne, 2022). A one-paragraph description in a publisher's catalog or an image on the cover may be enough to prevent a book from being purchased for a school. In many instances, the book is never read before a decision is made.

This soft censorship is particularly harmful in communities where students rely on their schools for most of their reading materials. Kids miss opportunities to read books that might resonate with them because the adults around them have decided to prevent this. When we deliberately deny students access to stories and voices that reflect their experiences, we communicate to them that their stories do not matter. We communicate they are not worthy of inclusion in the library—and it follows at school. Any time a book is removed to "protect" kids, the opposite happens: It harms kids who need that book the most.

School and Classroom Libraries Are Under Scrutiny

Because of organized efforts to remove books that contain the accurate and authentic stories and experiences of marginalized people, many librarians and teachers are under siege. Every week, colleagues contact us because the books in their classroom have fallen under scrutiny. What should teachers and librarians striving to offer relevant books do when uninformed people question those books? Too many teachers and librarians are simply removing them and storing them in a closet or taking them home. At more than one school we know, teachers' entire classroom collections have been packed up and stored off campus.

> Because of organized efforts to remove books that contain the accurate and authentic stories and experiences of marginalized people, many librarians and teachers are under siege.

Librarian educator and administrator, Jennifer LaGarde, has created a comprehensive, well-resourced guide for librarians and classroom teachers to develop a book selection policy at their schools and fight censorship challenges in their communities (find A Proactive Approach to Book Challenges at librarygirl.net). Take a proactive stance and develop your book selection criteria and processes *before* someone challenges the books in your school. Ask administrators about your district's book selection policies, too. Frequently there are policies or book selection criteria in place that are not followed because administrators override them or educators are not aware that district policies exist (Hixenbaugh, 2022).

The connection between bigotry and book challenges complicates efforts to increase book access for students. In many communities, educators are working together to educate the public about how books are selected and used in their schools. Becky Calzada, the library coordinator for Leander ISD, a large suburban district outside Austin, works to support librarians and teachers dealing with book challenges in her district and across Texas. Along with other librarians and library administrators, Becky is one of the leaders of the #FReadom campaign to support Texas school librarians and students' rights to read freely. In our interview with Becky, she offers advice to teachers, librarians, and administrators who are facing book challenges and censorship efforts in their schools.

COMMONSENSE SUGGESTIONS

Addressing Book Challenges and Censorship

Becky Calzada

Donalyn: In your school district, librarians and teachers have worked to diversify their collections and reading selections to include more voices and perspectives than the traditional "classics" their parents might have read. How have parents' expectations about what kids should be reading changed? Now it seems there is a backlash toward books that feature marginalized people. Your district has dealt with book challenges this school year. Could you tell us a little bit about what is happening?

Becky: First, not all parents believe that their kids should read the classics. There are parents who are avid readers, and I typically see kids following their example. You can tell when reading is an important part of the family's life. When a parent asks whether you, the school librarian, have the newest Jason Reynolds book, you know they are tuned in!

[As Becky points out, many parents and caregivers want their children and teens to read books about a wide variety of experiences, voices, cultures, and perspectives. They want their kids to read current, relevant, culturally responsive books. The people currently pushing book challenges in many communities do not represent the values or beliefs of many parents and members of our communities. However, many educators and librarians feel threatened and powerless when the school library and classroom libraries fall under scrutiny.]

What You Can Do About Censorship and Book Banning

Colby: What would you say to a teacher who sees all of this as really scary? We're not trained to evaluate books in the same ways that you librarians are. We teachers see all these banned book lists and hear about these books being censored. And that is an immediate trigger for us to just take these books off the shelf, because it's easier than to have to deal with all of this. Why is it important that we don't just remove the books?

Becky: I would probably tell that teacher there's a name for that—soft censorship. I can relate and understand that pain and empathize... I think about the kids who can see themselves, or maybe can't see themselves in the books. And so, what are the potential implications of banning books that could impact a group of kids, a group of readers?

I would also say, let me help you, because I think there's a way for us to navigate this by partnering and being transparent. I've heard of so many language arts teachers or teams that have said, "We want to take on this unit, so we are going to be extra transparent." They will give the parents a list of the titles, the unit instructional goals, and the summaries, and encourage parents to read them in advance, and they do a tremendous amount of groundwork. What can we do as librarians to support this work? How can we partner together? Because yes, it can be very fearful and scary, but I also know, too, there are so many resources out there for teachers.

[Many middle and high school teachers, Donalyn included, have written introductory letters to parents and caregivers, explaining the classroom library and students' freedom to choose books for independent reading. Such letters emphasize the broad range of readers the collection serves. If a reader is not emotionally mature enough for the book, or parents prefer their child doesn't read the book, that is fine. Parents have the right to decide what their children read. However, their jurisdiction does not extend to other people's children. Becky encourages teachers to be proactive about communicating with parents regarding the books available for their kids to read and to empower kids to abandon books they are not interested in reading.]

Becky: We tell parents, "We teach kids that if it's not a good fit, put it down. If you don't agree with the topic, it's okay." Then we are there to help them find something else to read. I have put books down, and it's no big deal. It's teaching an important life skill. Of course, teachers and librarians are always laying the groundwork for that conversation. How do you communicate with a parent in a way that is going to be productive and respectful?

Becky and other librarians recommend the professional resources listed here as credible sources of information and advocacy for librarians and teachers dealing with censorship and book banning in their schools and classrooms.

Resources for Fighting Censorship

- **The American Library Association's Library Bill of Rights**

- **The American Library Association Office of Intellectual Freedom's Ideas and Resources List**

- **The National Council of Teachers of English's Standing Committee Against Censorship**

- **The National Coalition Against Censorship's Resources for Teachers, Parents, and School Officials**

Search for these resources by name for more information.

3. Currency and Relevance

Ensuring that students have access to a wide variety of voices, perspectives, experiences, and points of view is just part of creating an effective classroom library. Students need accurate information, stories, and voices that relate authentically to their experiences. But it can be challenging to stay abreast of the newest books and downright impossible to evaluate all books. This section will help.

Forging relationships with your public and school librarians not only supports your students—it can also increase your book knowledge tenfold. Literacy expert Franki Sibberson reflects on what she learned about the relationship between the school library and the classroom library when she moved from the classroom to the library and back to the classroom.

COMMONSENSE SUGGESTIONS

Connecting the School Library and the Classroom
Franki Sibberson

Donalyn: Franki, you have worked as a teacher, then a librarian, then a teacher again. How did your classroom library change after you spent so many years in the library? Did you approach it differently?

Franki: What I realized when I was in the school library was that as a classroom teacher, I needed to know the school library really well in order to best serve my kids. I realized that what the school library collection carries are the books the kids in the school read. I intentionally connected with the school library collection better, and I took more responsibility to not just rely on the books we had in our classroom, but to also know the books available for my students in the school library.

As a teacher, I had my own books and I took care of my own reading. When I became a librarian, I realized that 90 percent of teachers and kids in a building rely on what's in the school library.

They don't go to the bookstore every Saturday. The school library builds the culture of the building. So classroom libraries and the school library are both important and must be connected.

Donalyn: Well, you know, when I was a new teacher, I didn't have a lot of books, so I checked out 100 books at a time from the public library. I would bring them down to school, and the kids and I would read them. I would do that with the school library, too, because it enhanced the collection that I had in my room. Reading a lot of library books taught me about so many books and authors. I learned a lot because of the scarcity of resources in my room. It drove me to seek other sources.

Meaningful book access has nothing to do with who owns the books. It's about proximity to the kids. Get the books to the kids by any means possible. Snobbery about credentials does not value kids' reading experiences outside of school, either. The most significant influences on the development of lifelong reading habits may be the least informed, but the most crucial adults of all—children's and teens' parents and caregivers (Scholastic, 2019). Partner with your librarian if you are lucky enough to have one at your school. Check out some rotating collections for book clubs or inquiry units and offer the books to expand students' choices. Talk with families about the literacy rituals and heritage they would like their children to experience at school.

Building Your Book Knowledge

If you're familiar with our educator blog, The Nerdy Book Club, you know that we read a lot of children's and young-adult literature. The two of us love to read and share books. Reading widely increases our book knowledge of the types of books available for kids and the writers and illustrators who create them. Our reading experiences inform our recommendations to other teachers, librarians, and caregivers, too. We don't promote books we do not read or have not talked about with a kid.

It is impossible to keep up with the slew of new books that come out each year. It is even difficult to scratch the surface. Like you, we want the *good* books. We want the best books for our students and the young people in our lives that we can find. We aspire to increase our book knowledge every year while accepting that we cannot read everything. We both admit to buying books we never read. We have busy lives, and sometimes we read less—just like all readers. Teaching, caregiving, or just living cut into our reading time.

The two of us know we need to read widely to keep up with our students' needs and our own professional development, and we try to keep it fun for ourselves. After all, we can't really sell kids on reading when it feels like work to us! Accept that you cannot read everything, and don't feel guilty about it. Feed yourself as a reader so that you can honestly model a reading life, which includes sharing your preferences and challenges. You don't need to read every children's book in the world to suggest books to children.

> Accept that you cannot read everything and don't feel guilty about it. Feed yourself as a reader, so you can honestly model a reading life….

If you want to build your book knowledge, start with the kids in front of you. Kidwatching is one of the best instructional habits we have. What are your students reading? What are they avoiding reading? Why? What gaps do you see in their reading lives? What gaps do you see in your own? What books are popular because the kids have made them viral?

When conferring with kids, listening to student book talks, or chatting with them about books, take their suggestions! Write down the books they tell you about, and make every effort to read as many of them as you can. Watch for books the kids are passing between them without your encouragement. Any book that becomes popular with several kids in the same class is a book worth moving to the top of your to-read pile! It clearly has kid appeal for your students. The two of us catch up on a lot of our students' favorites during school vacations so that the books can remain in circulation during the school year.

Next, connect with other readers in your school. Foster a relationship with your librarian and other teachers who enjoy reading children's and young adult literature. Exchange suggestions. Pay attention to the books kids are reading in the grades above and below yours by talking with teachers of those grades or asking your librarian about grade-level trends and popular titles. Your students will not be interested in reading only books for your grade, and their reading abilities will vary quite a bit. You don't have to keep a classroom collection that encompasses three grade levels of materials, but a good range best meets your students' needs. Working knowledge of representative favorites and notable titles in other grades can help you better match kids with books.

Visit your local library and, if you don't already have one, get a library card. If you don't live in the same neighborhood as your school, yet want to use the library in your school's neighborhood, investigate whether you can get a library card as an educator. Some library systems have reciprocal agreements with other libraries near them so that patrons can use both. It is especially important to foster relationships with your local public librarians if you do not have a full-time librarian at your school. Introduce yourself to the youth librarian and tell them what sorts of books your students want. Solicit their recommendations. Find out which resources are available for children and teens. Request books you discover that the library does not have in its collection. Librarians will assist you in locating books through interlibrary loan and might add your suggestions to their own purchasing lists. Your school and the local library are serving the same community, and working together makes sense for kids and families.

The two of us are connected to a wide community of book reviewers, bloggers, professional organizations (such as ALA and NCTE), publishers, authors, illustrators, and educators online. Beyond our reader-to-reader relationships with colleagues, students, and our families, there's our online reading community, which expands our book knowledge tremendously.

Talk with your school and local librarians about the professional review publications to which they subscribe. *The Horn Book, Booklist*, and *School Library Journal* are three of the most well-known publications, but many professional educator and librarian organizations create recommended lists of children's and young-adult literature, too. Check organizations beyond the language arts. For example, both the National Science Teaching Association (NSTA) and National Council for the Social Studies (NCSS) compile annual lists of the best trade books for their content areas and offer these lists for members.

Explore amateur review sites from well-respected reviewers. Ask colleagues on social media or in your school who they follow and read. Ensure that you are seeking out review sources led by educators and scholars of color, such as the Brown Bookshelf, Cotton Quilts, and the American Indians in Children's Literature blog. Later in this chapter, we list a few sources you might explore. As two white people who publicly review books, we recognize that the review community is dominated by white reviewers. To better serve kids and

Colby's fifth graders had a blast visiting their local public library: a librarian read them a story, they browsed the shelves, and they checked out books.

their books, educators need more inclusive and representative voices and sources of information. Never rely on just one source for book advice, no matter how good. To the degree possible, determine whether the reviewer receives paid sponsorships for promoting books or running ads. How does this affect their credibility? Use multiple sources of information and cross-check reviews when making purchasing and borrowing lists. Which titles are receiving favorable reviews from several sources— both professional and amateur? Which books seem like a good fit for your students or your curriculum? You do not need to read every notable or well-reviewed book, but you can keep up with big trends and highly recommended books by following reliable review sources online.

Make note of the authors and illustrators of this year's buzzworthy books and research their other works. Perhaps your school library or public library has copies of their earlier books. You can build your knowledge of the authors and illustrators writing books for kids today by investigating and reading their body of work—even when you cannot buy or track down their newest books, yet. Try some of these authors and illustrators with kids to determine interest. Then, narrow your list of new purchases to the creators that resonate with your kids this year.

Read representative titles from popular and well-regarded authors, illustrators, and series. You do not need to read every "I Survived" book to recommend the series to kids. You do not need to read every Jacqueline Woodson book to recommend her work to kids. Familiarize yourself with noteworthy titles that meet students' needs and interests. How would you use their books with students? For mentor texts?

Read-alouds? Book clubs? Independent reading choices? Which books reflect the author's craft and writing style? Which books have wide appeal? Seek out authors and illustrators that represent a variety of backgrounds, cultures, perspectives, experiences, genres, formats, stories, and topics.

Read evergreen titles that endure in popularity, too. The two of us remind ourselves that any book is new to the person who hasn't read it yet. In your efforts to build your book knowledge, don't just focus on new books all the time. While it is true that some books remain popular because adult nostalgia keeps them in print, there are many older books that remain interesting to kids. Every year, Colby has students who love Gary Paulsen's *Hatchet*, Christopher Paul Curtis's *Bud, Not Buddy*, or Kate DiCamillo's *Because of Winn-Dixie*. By reading as widely as we possibly can, we keep our own reading lives interesting and significantly increase our ability to connect kids with books.

Evaluating Books

Looking at books with a critical eye requires a lot of education and experience. Determining whether a book contains accurate representation and information, is of high quality, *and* will engage kids is a tall order for any teacher. When Donalyn informally polled teachers and librarians during a recent workshop, most of them reported they had taken only one or two children's and young-adult literature courses in their teacher-education programs. Educators with advanced degrees in literacy topics may have attended one or two more. Unsurprisingly, school librarians received the most formal education in reading and evaluating children's and young-adult literature.

> You do not have to evaluate all the books in your classroom library by yourself, nor should you. Rely on the expert advice of librarians, reviewers, scholars, and publishers.

Good news: You do not have to evaluate all the books in your classroom library by yourself, nor should you. Rely on the expert advice of librarians, reviewers, scholars, and publishers. Through social media, teachers, librarians, and readers can often connect with the creators themselves—following authors and illustrators to find out the latest news on their work. Read as many books as you can and talk with school and online colleagues in person and online about the books they are reading and planning to read. Talk to your students, too, who will offer amazing insight into the books they read and the ones you share with them. Encourage them to offer their opinions about books as often and as informally as possible.

Donalyn displayed recent read-alouds on top of a bookcase in her fifth-grade classroom library. Kids were encouraged to write a few words about their impressions of each read-aloud on index cards and to stick their "reviews" on the cover. Kids not only benefit from their spontaneous and authentic responses, but also from looking at the books they read through different lenses. First, as a reader and child, as the author intended (Miller & Lesesne, 2022), then as a student who has learned a thing or two about books.

One of the big literacy events at Parma Elementary this year is the Mock Caldecott unit. All 400 or so students will be able to read 20 or so picture books and consider them for award contention. Colby uses this event and the conversations and reading around it to teach his readers more about looking at books with an evaluative eye.

Our Mock Caldecott Unit

The Caldecott Medal is awarded annually by the American Library Association to the illustrator of the most distinguished American picture book for kids. For years, my students participated in a mock Caldecott unit. Kids would spend weeks reading, studying, and discussing 20 great picture books published that year. In November, librarian and writer John Schu and I release our annual list of books for Mock Caldecott Awards, and many teachers and librarians use our lists for their own units or create Mock Caldecott lists of their own.

After studying and rating each book based on the Caldecott criteria I have shared with them, kids write persuasive arguments for their favorites. After presenting their arguments to the class, they vote on

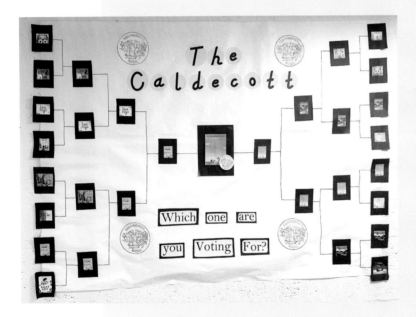

their choices for the Mock Caldecott Medal winner and Honor books. When the American Library Association announces the recipients of the Caldecott Medal and Honors (and many other awards) during its January livestream, my readers and I watch, eager to see whether any of our favorites were chosen by the committee. Kids are so invested in their books. It is fun and gratifying to see how excited they are when one of their favorites wins, the discussions that immediately spring from each announcement, and the verbal and nonverbal protests when a beloved book is snubbed by the committee! Most importantly, kids enjoy 20 deep reading experiences and learn more about books and reading.

This year, I wrote and received a grant for our school library that would provide all 20 of the Schu/Sharp Mock Caldecott books. It has been exciting to see this unit go from my 25 students in one class to the 400+ students in our entire building. Each week when classes come to the library, our librarian reads and discusses two books from the list. Then students record their favorite on a ballot and why they think the book is a winner. At the end of the week, the ballots are tallied, and the book with the most votes across the school moves on to the next round.

My fifth graders are not always thrilled on Friday afternoons when our secretary, Ms. Garver, announces the weekly winner over the intercom. When Brendan Wenzel's *Inside Cat* lost to Elisha Cooper's *Yes & No*, my class let out a collective groan. Remmy was not happy. He said, "I wonder if the other classrooms voted on the quality of the illustrations or if they just voted on the story that they liked best." Remmy's observation led to a great classroom discussion about what makes great art. I loved being able to celebrate these 20 beautiful picture books with all of the students of Parma Elementary. I can't wait to see how this project evolves in the years to come.

Teaching students to look at books through both personal and critical lenses supports their reading development and helps them find and evaluate books on their own. Teachers need a background in evaluating children's and young-adult books ourselves and resources we can rely on to provide accurate, unsponsored, critical reviews. When evaluating books for addition to classroom libraries, teachers must consider social and cultural representation and kid appeal first and foremost because the books are primarily used for independent reading and group reading activities, such as book clubs. Let's take a closer look at these important considerations.

Are the Books Appealing to Your Students?

Whether we want to admit it or not, there are a lot of books that adults buy that kids don't read. The two of us have purchased plenty of books for our students (and our children!) that we could not entice them to read. We cannot forget that children's and young-adult literature is written for children and young adults. While book-savvy teachers and librarians can locate, evaluate, and recommend books to students, independent reading is supposed to be self-selected, not teacher-directed. You can lead a reader to the shelves, but you cannot make them read.

When sharing resources with educators for locating books, our colleagues are often surprised to learn that many of the major book awards bestowed on children's and young-adult books do not consider kid appeal when selecting winners. This is one of the reasons we started the Nerdy Book Club blog years ago—we wanted to celebrate books that our students loved to read, whether they were "award-worthy" or not.

While we do want books of outstanding literary merit in our classroom libraries, we must remember that they are available in places other than our classroom libraries, such as at our school library and public library. When picking and choosing between books to buy or borrow, better to select books that you know will appeal to your students. Invite students to help you keep a running list of books you might add to the library. Colby keeps a list in a note on his phone, another list on a sheet of notebook paper in his conferring binder, and a third list on the whiteboard, where students add titles. When the whiteboard list gets too long, he snaps a photo of it and adds it to the note on his phone. Book talks and conferences provide more insight into kids' interests and preferences for books. Use student survey responses to identify trends across the class, and conference information to home in on individual reader's interests.

Work with your school librarian to locate books on topics of interest to your students. Familiarize yourself with series and authors that kids like. Pay attention to student conversations about books. Which books and topics are hot

One of the best ways to determine books that will appeal to your students is, of course, to ask your students.

this year? How have kids' interests changed? How can your classroom library evolve to accommodate shifts in student interest, popular culture, and the types of books being published for kids?

Can Your Students Read the Books?

When publishers identify age ranges and reading levels for their children's books, consider them ballpark ranges and levels, not hard-and-fast indicators of the age or ability of the kids who can read those books. In any classroom, you will find a wide range of readers—kids who read below, at, and above grade-level assessment measures; kids who lack sufficient background knowledge to comprehend a particular text; and so on. The format and design of a book—such as the amount of white space on a page or the font size—may present reading challenges for a reader (Miller & Sharp, 2018). Just because a book in a catalog proclaims to be a good fit for your fifth graders does not mean all your students will be able to read it (much less want to).

It does not matter how many books you keep in the classroom library if your students cannot read them. During a districtwide audit of classroom libraries, Maggie Hoddinott, Annie Ward, and their colleagues determined that many of the books in teachers' classroom libraries were too difficult for their students to read. These "de facto book deserts" were deceptive because the shelves were stuffed with books. Clearly access was prevalent! However, the collections did not offer the variety of reading levels and formats required to equitably support kids' reading development (Harvey & Ward, 2017). School libraries alone could not meet the demand.

While talking with Annie, Maggie, and Suzanne Carroll about the origins of their district's current classroom library and reading initiatives, they described teachers' and librarians' ongoing efforts to match kids with the right book at the right time. Across the district—for every student—book access remains a top priority, but such support requires effort and planning to maintain. In particular, Annie, Maggie, Suzanne and others have focused their attention and study toward the needs of students who are not yet reading proficiently for their age, but striving.

Launching and Sustaining Districtwide Classroom Library Initiatives

Annie Ward, Maggie Hoddinott, and Suzanne Carroll

Donalyn: I think your intentionality around what you're doing is so important for teachers and school leaders to learn about because it's one thing for us to describe matching kids with books in a classroom where it's going well, but that's not where it starts. It starts with a lot of years in a dusty book room trying to figure out what schools have in a closet that kids might read. Annie, how did your classroom library initiative start?

Annie: I came to Mamaroneck in 2004, and there were classroom libraries. There are so many assumptions that teachers, librarians, we all might make, and it's really at our peril.

When we make any assumption about access, it's flawed. Around 2014, I was looking carefully at striving readers and really getting granular. I have a practice, as many administrators do, of rotating in and out of classrooms and looking to see what's really going on—talking to kids. I was paying close attention to what books striving readers had in their hands and the way they would talk about what they were reading or not reading.

One of my findings was that the kid that teachers were worried about . . . is the kid who is roaming around with a book in a book baggie or a book box, but who is not actively reading, or who is not speaking about that book with enthusiasm.

Like anything else when you start paying attention, I got a theory, "Gee, I don't think our striving readers are finding great matches in our libraries." That's where the whole sweater unraveled because that's when I saw a desperate need for weeding. That's when I saw striver after striver unable to find or connect with books they could read. We had classroom libraries, but it was more a question of what types of books were in those libraries, and really viewing them through the eye of the striving reader that led me to realize that we had a massive problem.

Donalyn: The Scholastic Kids & Family Reading Report backs up your observations. Year after year, kids report that their caregivers underestimate how hard it is for them to find books to read (2019). We think just because we have a school library that our students know how to use one. We think a fifth grader knows how to consistently find a book in the library—they don't. We think an eighth grader knows—they don't. Even before COVID-19, kids weren't getting a lot of opportunities to browse books in the library. Kids need lots of time to preview, share, and talk about books they might read, not just books they are reading. As you have observed yourselves, a lot of the classroom talk between kids is discussing the books they are currently reading and the books they just finished.

But that vision of future reading is what we want kids to have. It seems that you are telling us that no matter how well-intentioned, the classroom libraries across your district did not equitably offer students a place where they could confidently and consistently find books to read.

[As Annie and her colleagues found, there was a mismatch between the reading abilities of their students and the books offered to them through classroom libraries. In spite of a decade of investment in classroom libraries, many collections did not meet the needs of the readers they served. Maggie explains how this mismatch affected the most fragile readers, in particular. Teachers need support and resources for building their book knowledge and evaluation skills, as well as funding for classroom books.]

Maggie: That was particularly the case for our striving readers. As Annie describes in *From Striving to Thriving*, I conducted a classroom library audit across all of our 125 classroom libraries. Lots of findings emerged from that, one of which was that we had beautiful classroom libraries with hundreds and hundreds, if not thousands, of books in each. But when you really got granular and looked at the books that were actually in the classrooms, and then layered on top the reading abilities of the kids in those classes, we found that in class after class after class, the collections were skewed high, and they favored the already proficient or even thriving readers. It's through Annie's relentless attention to the strivers that we were able to maintain this laserlike focus on ensuring that our classroom libraries are well-balanced and that they do meet the needs of the kids in the room.

[Maggie's description of classroom libraries filled with books that kids could not read reinforces the need for weeding and curating a collection with kids in mind. It does not matter how many books you have if your students cannot access the stories and information inside them. Furthermore, when administrators and community members see classroom and library shelves overflowing with books, they tend to question why more funding is needed for reading materials. Weeding reveals gaps in a collection and makes room for new materials in response to students' needs and interests.]

We're also starting to realize that there's the classroom library that attends to the needs of kids who have average interests and abilities for their age. Most of these kids are going to be able to find books in the classroom library. You're always going to have outliers. We have found that our students who are thriving readers, who are engaged and confident readers, very likely have access streams. Of course, we're never going to not attend to them and book-match with them. But we find they're finding books in the school library, their parents take them to the public library, they have books in the home, or they can go to other classrooms, and they find themselves books.

But if we don't pay attention to the striving readers on the other end of the spectrum—that's where we lose kids. And they don't accrue reading volume. So that's where we came up with some of the more systemic approaches to ensure that all our kids have a robust book access stream.

Districtwide Support and Resources

[Recognizing the need to increase equitable access to books for all children, district and school administrators have dedicated funding toward purchasing books and supporting school and classroom libraries. However, ensuring that all teachers have the same opportunity to add to their collections, keep current on new titles and trends, and build their ability to evaluate books is not easy to accomplish districtwide. Maggie explains how they began.]

Colby: I'm curious to know how you ensure there is book access in every classroom. Sometimes, it comes down to do you get the teacher with a lot of books? Or do you get the other teacher? I always think of what would happen if a kid had book access all the way through school with a teacher who was excited about reading. How do teachers get books? If you're a new teacher, what training do you have, so that you know how to talk about books?

Maggie: When I first started in the job, there was not a systematic approach across the district, Colby. Teachers who were agentive, who really took an interest in children's literature, had beautifully curated collections. Every classroom did have a collection, but they were curated to varying degrees. We looked at it through several lenses.

First, we did a lot of professional development with teachers, helping them to understand what we meant by volume. I think there was a big perception that what we were saying was just give them a book, and they'll be fine. On the capability side, of course, we need to teach kids the skills and strategies they need to be proficient readers. But we also need to pay attention to their volume, because if we don't give them authentic opportunities to put into practice those skills and strategies, we can't be surprised if they don't develop a love of reading or progress as readers. On the adaptive side, that was a positive change.

Donalyn: Your work with volume-based intervention has resulted in your students' increased reading skills, but self-selection proficiency also builds on itself. The more kids read—and the more successful they become in their choices—the more their book-selection abilities improve. Can you tell us how you have spread volume-based reading interventions across your district?

Suzanne: We've talked a lot about helping kids to build agency. We've tried to develop interventions or strategies and name them. Take the volume conference form, for example. That tool organically came about because we wanted to learn about our striving readers' lives, not just their decoding, fluency, and comprehension. Are you reading something? If you're not, what's the last thing you read? Where did you find it? When you create an assessment that teachers can use for every reader, it has more credibility. Teachers can identify whether a reader is an agentive reader or not.

Interventions are traditionally connected to small-group and guided reading instruction. Kids need that support. That work was not connected to our volume-based intervention. Teachers didn't see the value. Maggie and I talked with them and learned that some were hearing messages that they didn't need to conduct small-group instruction anymore. Just give them books, and they'll be fine! Teachers felt that their expertise was devalued. We attended campus meetings and assured teachers that kids need both.

[As Suzanne emphasized, students benefit from good reading instruction and increasing their reading volume. When kids read more, they enjoy reading more and invest more time doing it (Scholastic, 2019).]

Volume Conference Form

STUDENT: Nigel		DATE: 2/12
TEACHER: Ms. Driver		
QUESTION	**RESPONSE**	**POSSIBLE NEXT STEPS**
What are you currently reading?	• Children's Encyclopedia of Facts	
How did you find this book?	• Classroom library • Has had in his book box for 3 days	
How do you usually find books?	• Classroom library	• Teach other sources for finding books. • What are his access streams?
What is this book making you think about?	• Learning interesting facts (shared a fact about Neptune).	• Was not aware that book is organized alphabetically. Teach about book structure.
Do you have a plan for finishing this book?	I'm not sure yet.	• Observe for minutes spent reading each day and level of engagement/investment.
Do you know what book you're going to read next?	No.	• Confer about ways to find books. • Start "next up" book list
How much time do you spend reading in school?	I read during independent reading time.	• Discuss other times to read (ex. morning; packup)
How much time do you spend reading at home?	• I try to read for 20 minutes each night. • Reading "The One and Only Ivan" at home	• Bring in "The One and Only Ivan" to confer • May need to make reading pla
Does anything get in the way of your at-home reading?		
Is there anything else you would like me to know about you as a reader?		
And space for notes at the bottom]		

NOTES:
• Schedule 1:1 conference and determine if "The One and Only Ivan" is a good match.

The form Annie, Maggie, and Suzanne use in reading conferences to gain a deeper understanding of students' interests, preferences, habits, and access streams

Maggie: On the technical side, we looked at how the budgeting was allocated across the district. When we started to look at the unique needs in every building and every classroom, we saw that the needs were very different. We have a dual-language program, and the kids in the dual-language program are going back and forth between classes. So one classroom library would have 48 kids shopping from it, as opposed to a general classroom that might have 20 or 24 kids. Plus, students needed Spanish books and English books. We realized that the dual-language teacher needs twice the amount of money to purchase books because her classroom library has to be twice as large.

Annie: The first thing we found was that principals were not allocating money directly to teachers in any kind of consistent fashion. This was really a problem. Book money was commingled with supply money. We had to find where the funding was and make sure that it wasn't being diverted into new, fabulous foam cube seating outside the library. Then, there was nothing in the library because stuff was being spent on furniture. I mean, literally, it was that bad.

Maggie: We started doing a little bit of forensic accounting in terms of where money was going and how it was best distributed. The principals do get a per-pupil allocation for their campus. A separate pot goes directly to teachers now. There's a tiered system. Classroom teachers receive $500, integrated co-teach classrooms get $750, and dual-language classrooms receive $1,000. The special education teachers' classes or special education classes may only include eight to 12 students, but these classrooms also receive $500 a year because they teach such a range of reading interests and abilities. Everyone receives funds for books, including specialists, art and music teachers— everybody has money to purchase books.

[Funding classroom libraries for every teacher in the building, as well as the school library, sends a powerful message about the value system in a school. Reading is clearly considered an important skill and entry point to learning across disciplines, content-area literacy is valued and supported, and classroom libraries can better represent the readers in your school and their needs and interests in ways that a one-size-fits-all boxed library cannot. Maggie describes this balance between creating equal collections across a school or district and customizing your classroom library for your students each year.]

Keeping the Collections Relevant and Current

Maggie: We encourage you to build your library for the readers you usually teach. So, if I'm a third-grade teacher, I expect kids to read in this range, and I expect they're going to be into disasters, survival, animals, and some go-to series. I'm going to curate the library for a typical third-grade class, but I am going to customize any purchases with my yearly budget allocation for the readers each year who need different books.

The third book budget pot stays with the district literacy team. Every year I put together a classroom library "infusion" for each grade that includes newly published titles. This really gives us a chance to bring some consistency across the district to our classroom libraries, and to add some current books each year to our classroom libraries. If I'm not a teacher who's curating my collection, a kid in that teacher's classroom is still going to have access to new, noteworthy, and diverse texts.

Well-meaning adults often unwittingly limit students' book access by creating "de facto book deserts" or adding few new books to collections, but there is one way adults deliberately limit access: censorship.

Weeding Books

While we often think of acquiring books as the main work of building a strong classroom library, it is just as important to consider which books you might need to get rid of. While it might seem that it's always better to have more books, it's better to have a smaller collection with books that actually appeal to readers in your classroom than to have overflowing shelves of dated or worn books about topics that don't interest kids. Readers are less likely to find a book matching their interests with such unappealing books in front of them. Over time, some will stop searching—convinced that finding a book they might like is too hard or, perhaps, that no books interest them. Additionally, weeding worn and outdated books from your collections gives you a better understanding of which books you need to enhance and expand students' access and provide books they will want to read.

As you weed, consider the unique needs, interests, and identities of the readers in your classroom. What gaps do you notice as you align what you know about your students with what you see on your shelves? Consider including students in the weeding process. Their opinions about and experiences with books, and the extent to which those books do or don't appeal to them, can help you curate a collection that will engage them.

Like many teachers, Donalyn spent the first few years of her teaching career acquiring as many books for her classroom library as she could—scrounging for books at garage sales and discount stores, taking donations from families or retiring teachers, and occasionally buying new books from a school supply catalog or book fair.

> Consider including students in the weeding process. Their opinions about and experiences with books, the extent to which those books do or don't appeal to them, can help you curate a collection that will engage them.

After 10 years, the classroom library held thousands of books. There were a lot of good books in the collection—thoughtfully researched and chosen. There were also many books that just collected—books that were worn or damaged, outdated, or lacked kid appeal. Such books were dust magnets at best. At worst, the unread books prevented kids from finding books. When kids must dig through uninteresting books, they are less likely to find one they want to read. Over time, kids will stop trusting the classroom library as an access point because it is full of ugly, old books, or it makes finding a good book too challenging. Donalyn knew she needed to get rid of some books, but deciding what needed to go was overwhelming. Throwing away books was painful. What if a kid discovered Brian Jacques's Redwall series and wanted to read all 17? She might need them! Any teacher who has invested a lot of money and time building a classroom library can relate to how she felt.

MUSTIE Shows the Way

If your school or district provides funding for classroom library books, request a percentage for replacing worn, damaged, or lost books. When a book wears out or goes missing, think about whether kids still read it before replacing it.

For a way to evaluate the classroom library equitably and logically, several librarian colleagues suggested MUSTIE, a list of factors to consider when evaluating and weeding a school library collection (Larson, 2021). Although school librarians have many considerations when curating a large collection such as the school library, teachers can use MUSTIE as a checklist for evaluating the condition and currency of their classroom libraries. MUSTIE is defined as:

Misleading. Information is not static. Humankind continues to evolve, discover new information, and interrogate our past interpretations. The world changes. Our understanding of the world changes, too. Books in a collection that were accurate when added to the library may be outdated or inaccurate now. Books identifying Pluto as a planet or Barack Obama as the current president of the United States mislead young people with inaccurate information.

In addition to looking at the condition of books, consider whether the content communicates biased viewpoints or incomplete information. Books that contain stereotypes about a particular group or person present misleading information, too. Books about colonization that do not include the perspectives of Indigenous people who were forced off their lands would be misleading, for example. Children would not receive an accurate overview of this historical period from the perspectives of all people involved. Use resources such as Lee and Low's Checklist: 8 Steps to Creating a Diverse Book Collection and Teaching for Change's Guide for Selecting Anti-Bias Children's Books. Seek out professional development about dismantling biases and evaluating children's and young adult literature.

Ugly. Books wear out with use. Consider books consumable materials that should not last for decades. If kids are reading them, the books will fall apart. If you want your classroom library books to remain clean and pristine, keep kids away from the books at all costs. Yes, teachers can set the expectation that kids help take care of the books and keep them in good shape. We must be realistic, though. Putting books in kids' hands means that some will come back sticky.

Donalyn finds a good example of an "ugly" book in Colby's classroom.

Beyond physical condition, kids will often reject a book if the cover looks old-fashioned—even your beloved childhood copy of *Sarah, Plain and Tall*. The 90's cover looks ugly to your fifth graders, not nostalgic. Some books have evergreen appeal from one generation to the next—but while that is true, if the cover or book design looks dated, many kids won't pick it up. Examine covers for kid appeal, and ask a few students if you are uncertain. Weed the least appealing. Publishers often change covers, fonts, and back matter for updated editions of popular books so that the books express timeless appeal.

Superseded. A book is superseded when there is a new edition or a better resource on the subject available. Weed books when you acquire updated editions. Reprints of books often include new information, fresh covers and design elements, as well as resources such as book-club guides. If you have multiple copies of a book and need to weed for space, remove the oldest editions (even if they are in better condition) to ensure accuracy and currency.

Trivial: Determining whether a book is trivial considers young people's opinions, not adults'. Books that are trivial are not interesting to the reading community using the library—not a judgment of the books' value. Will students read this book or not? In Texas, Donalyn doesn't need many books about cross-country skiing in the classroom library. Her students have not shown much interest. She has bought a lot of books about soccer over the years, though.

Sometimes, the two of us have purchased or tracked down books about niche topics of interest for the benefit of one kid or a group of kids during one school year. The next year, no one read them. To weed or not? When in doubt, book-talk it. Do any kids show interest? Does the book have curricular value? Can you use it for a lesson somehow? If not, it is not worth the shelf space.

Irrelevant: Determining whether a book is irrelevant often means evaluating shifting interests in popular culture—such as celebrities or movie tie-ins. Kids' tastes change. Often, kid culture trends flow from older kids to younger ones. Perhaps earlier grades will enjoy your books about narwhals and sloths when the next animal fad arrives in your classroom!

Elsewhere: You do not need to store every award-winning title or the complete runs of popular series in your classroom. The collection is meant to supplement other resources, not to provide a comprehensive reading assortment for all students. If students need or want a title you do not have, work with your school and public librarians to locate it or check with other schools in your district. Most public libraries purchase the winners of awards such as the Newbery, Caldecott, Coretta Scott King, Printz, National Book Award, and other notable literary awards for young people. Request that your library purchase award-winning books and books from notable lists, especially books written and illustrated by marginalized creators, so that more children have access to these stories and voices.

As for popular series, consider how many children show interest and how many books you can reasonably store in one or two tubs at most. Instead of purchasing all of the books in a long series, Donalyn often purchased duplicates of the first few books, which are in the highest demand. If kids wanted to keep reading a longer series, she helped them locate later books through the library (or other sources).

Criteria for weeding, like MUSTIE and others, provide a general framework for evaluating your classroom library books to determine their currency and condition. Ultimately, you are the final word on whether a book should be weeded.

How Can I Get Rid of Our Books?

Invite a colleague to weed your classroom library with you, and offer to help weed theirs. Let them get first dibs on any books you are giving away. You have veto power over the books in your classroom. You can always keep books your colleague recommends weeding if you have your own reasons for keeping them. But don't feel guilty about throwing away or donating books you no longer need for your students.

Classroom space is finite. There are only so many books kids can reasonably browse. Building a classroom library is not about displaying a tasteful, Instagram-worthy collection of the best children's books. A classroom library, like any library, is meant for readers to use. Kids' interests change. New books are published. You will never reach a place where your classroom library is perfect. Libraries grow and change in response to their readers. You will never be finished. As new books come into the collection, you will reach a tipping point. Some books must go.

Donate books that do not interest your students after two or three years. Book-talk overlooked books and try to generate interest. If no one takes a chance on a book, consider whether it is a better fit for another grade level. Colby's school has a giveaway table at the front of the school for families and teachers to give and take books for kids to read.

If a book is not worth keeping in the classroom, think long and hard before donating it to other kids. Why would you pass along a damaged or antiquated book?

Throwing away books is difficult, especially if you purchased the books or brought them from home.

When Donalyn was a classroom teacher, she often repurposed MUSTIE books by using them to make bookmarks.

Consider what we communicate to kids when the books we offer have ripped pages, ancient covers, and musty smells. Such books do not entice kids to read!

If you feel guilty about throwing books away, consider recycling them or using them for writing and craft projects. Tear out pages and use them for blackout poetry or artwork. Donalyn lined bulletin boards with old book pages and cut them into strips for bookmarks. Add old books and dust jackets to your crafting supplies or donate them to an artist or crafter. A quick search on Etsy and Pinterest found abundant ideas for repurposing books into everything from wrapping paper to handbags!

A Sidenote About Replacing Books

In the early stages of my classroom library development, I used all the funds and bonuses I had (money from the district, grants, PTA, Scholastic Book Club points, personal money, and so on) to buy books. As soon as the money was at my disposal, I would buy books to add to our classroom library. Now that my library has grown to somewhere between two and three thousand books, I am not in the same kind of rush to purchase books. When the school year starts, many of the books in our classroom library are new to my readers, so adding books to our collection can wait. Instead, I try to know my readers better and learn what they want. My district currently gives all K–5 teachers $250 a year to purchase books for our classroom library. I wait until about halfway through the school year to spend this money.

During his midyear book order, Colby purchased books that his students had requested, as well as books he thought they would be excited to read.

If a hot new release comes out, the next book in a popular series drops, or we are missing a needed book, I often just purchase those books with my own money. That ends up accounting for two to five books each month.

Newly published books and books that match my current students' interests take priority over replacing older books. Often, when a book is worn out, kids are no longer reading it, and I do not need to buy another copy. When deciding which books to replace, I purchase the books that students want to read most:

- **Early books in a chronological series.** When a popular series is missing Book #2, many kids stop reading all of the books. By replacing one missing or damaged book, you can renew interest in the whole set.

- **Popular books by a favorite author.** Certain authors are perennial favorites for my fifth graders every year, such as Kwame Alexander and Lynda Mullaly Hunt. If we lose a book from one of kids' favorite authors, I will replace it if I can.

- **Graphic novels.** The paper used for graphic novels is heavy, and the bindings rarely hold up to lots of readers. When popular titles such as Raina Telgemeier's *Smile* or Dav Pilkey's *Dog Man* start to lose their pages, I add them to the replacement list.

Books are consumable items. They do not last forever. Prioritize replacing the books your students are most interested in reading. Teachers need funding support for replacing classroom library books that remain popular with students year after year. Work with your school librarian to determine which high-interest, evergreen titles are available in the school library. Remember MUSTIE: Books that are available "Elsewhere" may not need replacement if kids can easily locate them.

Award-winning administrator Don Vu recognizes that successful independent reading and classroom library initiatives require sustained support from school administrators. Working with colleagues and families to develop more current and engaging book collections for kids, Dr. Vu has identified his most important suggestions for school principals who want to support classroom libraries.

Five Ways Principals Can Support Classroom Libraries

By Don Vu

As a principal, you yield great influence over the culture and vision of your school. Literacy leaders who are really committed to creating a culture of reading know that a critical piece of that effort is to ensure that all classrooms have vibrant and engaging libraries. Here are five tips for principals as you build and grow classroom libraries.

1 **Professional learning.** The first step isn't to buy more books. The first step is to plan engaging and transformative professional development for your staff. If you want to create lifelong readers, you will need teachers and staff who are passionate about reading and books. They also need to know which books are available and noteworthy. Collaborate with a local chapter of a reading association to bring authors and other literacy leaders to your campus. Beyond traditional "sit and get" trainings, consider sending teachers to a local book festival, reading conference, or author reading at a bookstore. These can be informative and fun, and they can spark the love of reading and books in adults!

2 **Student voice and choice.** Nope, you're still not ready to buy more books. As a staff, you'll want to find ways to understand and track student interests. What are their hobbies? What are they curious about? Who are their favorite authors? Research tells us (which Donalyn and Colby explain in this book) that student choice is a critical consideration for classroom libraries. In my former school, we used to give each student an interest inventory before making big purchases for our classroom libraries, just to ensure we choose the right books.

3 **Remember windows and mirrors.** Just one more thought before you set up those purchase orders! Your classroom libraries should give students a chance to widen their horizons and allow them to see different perspectives and ideas, as well as explore the far reaches of the world. Those books should also give students a chance to see themselves reflected in the stories shared. The stories that we choose to share reflect what we value and honor. Be sure that your classroom libraries are diverse in the way our world is diverse.

continued next page

4 **Show me the money.** Okay, go ahead and buy the books now. Wait, you don't have the money? This is probably the most common issue that principals mention when considering classroom libraries. My solution: PRIORITIZE. As you commit, you'll need to prioritize and allocate money to purchase books before anything else. Think of books like you think of pencils. You can't have school without them. Use carry-over money (which we all have at the end of the year) to fund conferences, software, and other less essential items. Additionally, you may also find ways to partner with literacy organizations, booksellers, and local libraries and businesses to help get more books into classrooms.

5 **Celebrate the joy of reading.** While independent reading should be an important part of your curriculum, books and stories should be seen as the "fun" stuff. With this mentality, you should ensure that there is a lot of celebration and joy when planning and outfitting classroom libraries. Book-talk the new books. Think of exciting ways to engage kids in the celebration of stories. Share books with one another! You can have great classroom libraries, but it doesn't matter much if kids aren't having fun reading the books!

School and district leaders support young readers when they become enthusiastic advocates for students' rights to positive reading experiences and meaningful book access.

4. Organization and Use

You can curate a current and relevant classroom library filled with interesting books, but if students cannot locate the books they want, what's the point? Because every classroom space and community differs, teachers must remain flexible and focus on kids' interactions. Two students won't approach the classroom library in the same way because of their past experiences and their feelings of confidence and safety in your classroom. There is no right way to organize or use your classroom library— just find the way that works best for your students and you. By reflecting on your students' behaviors and being realistic about your limitations for the collection, you can transform your classroom library into a space that invites kids into reading and helps you keep your books under reasonable control. You cannot change the size of your classroom, where the windows are located, or how high your students can comfortably reach for a book. Limitations such as those should control how your books are stored and displayed.

Organizing the Library Space and Books

Now that you have weeded the classroom library, you can identify how many books you have left in the collection and the space available to store and display books in your classroom. Once you determine where you can keep the books, it is time to consider how to organize the collection. Kids will need to be able to find and return books, and you will want to keep the books from taking over the room.

While many librarians are familiar with S. R. Ranganathan's classic "Five Laws of Library Use" and the modern variations, few teachers know about these fundamental beliefs about libraries and books. As you think about your classroom library's organization, let those laws guide you.

Strive for Responsiveness, Not Perfection

There's no such thing as perfect classroom library organization when you have kids in the room. You are not running a book museum. Libraries need readers. Readers are sticky. They use wrappers for bookmarks. (Hey, it's better than dog-earing the pages!) Sometimes, readers don't put books back where they belong. Sometimes, books are lost. Sometimes, the shelves and bins are a mess. You are building a classroom library for kids, not for Instagram! If it looks too perfect, the two of us would wonder how often kids were free to use it.

You will never reach a place where your classroom library is "done," unless it is the day before your last

The Five Laws of Library Use

1 **Books are for use.** Books are meant to be read. Children's books are meant to be read by children. No paperback book has been designed that can survive 100 kids reading it. Books will get damaged, lost, or wear out.

2 **Every reader their book.** Each reader is unique and develops their own tastes and preferences. Classroom libraries are judgment-free zones designed to engage kids with reading, not control their reading choices.

3 **Every book its reader.** While you want to offer books with wide appeal, there is room for a few books that interest a smaller group of kids—sometimes just one.

4 **Save the time of the reader.** Anticipate and address obstacles to library use that diminish readers' abilities to find books. Talk with students about what they like about the classroom library and what makes it challenging to use.

5 **The library is a growing organism.** Your classroom collection must evolve to support your student and curriculum's evolving needs.

—S. R. Ranganathan

day of teaching. Even after retirement, you might run into a former student who still has one of your books. One of Donalyn's colleagues had this experience at Target! You will acquire and weed books in a cyclical fashion forever. Kids will come and go. Their tastes will change, and so will the books published for them. Watching kids as they use the library and interact with the books and each other will tell you a lot about whether your organization system is working or not. Colby invested some time recently in watching his students as they moved around the library to determine whether the traffic flow was leading kids to books or making it more challenging for them to access areas of the library.

Observing Kids Move in the Classroom Library

I spend a lot of time trying to make sure that our classroom library traffic flow doesn't interfere with anything else going on in our classroom. During the middle of the school year, I decided it would be a good time to assess how things were going with the flow. I hadn't noticed any specific issues lately, but it is always good to check in a couple of times a year to make sure things are moving smoothly. Donalyn and I talked about traffic flow when we were reorganizing the library over the summer, and we recently discussed how it was going with kids. I planned to spend a week kidwatching the traffic flow around the bookshelves and library spaces to see how much time kids were spending in the classroom library and anything else interesting I noticed. Holy smokes! I noticed something fascinating. My students were spending hardly any noticeable time in our classroom library. Of course, I didn't witness every student's interaction with the classroom library because I was busy teaching, conferring, working with groups, and chatting with kids about our recent field trip to a ski resort. But I did witness these things:

- Kids spent between 10 and 30 seconds in the classroom library. They were not going to the classroom library to browse at this point in the school year—they were going to get a specific book to read. They knew exactly where to find it by now and didn't linger.

- Often when I saw a reader grab a book from the classroom library, they would bring it to another reader—either a friend or a tablemate. This was exciting! Kids were talking about books with each other, and those conversations were leading them to recommend books. The library was still an important resource, but kids were becoming a powerful resource to each other.

- The intentionality invested into the classroom library pays off for kids. The time invested in organizing the classroom library and helping kids understand it and understand themselves as readers increased their confidence and ability to self-select books. Kids spent less time looking for books and more time recommending and talking about books with their classmates.

The last student I observed in the classroom library that week was Ava. It was Friday afternoon, and Ava needed a book for the weekend. She'd been reading a lot since the beginning of the year, but recently she had increased her reading dramatically. A switch flipped, and she was burning through a 200-page book almost daily. She grabbed *Wild Survival Crocodile Rescue!* by Melissa Cristina Márquez. Ava's trip to the library lasted roughly three seconds. She knew exactly what she wanted and how to find it, and she snatched it up.

I told Ava that I was curious about why she decided to take that book. She told me that she saw the title of the second book in the Wild Survival series written on the BOOKS WE NEED TO BUY list in our classroom. This running list is a spot for kids to add books they think we need. She thought that if someone in our class enjoyed the first book so much that we needed the second one, she should check it out.

I never in a million years thought that the list of books we needed to buy would lead to a student reading a book that we already had in our classroom library. All of the things that we do to build community and help readers are interrelated. Whether we know it or not, every decision we make has the potential to lead a reader toward or away from reading.

The most important feature of any classroom library is the readers who use it. Without them, it does not matter what books are in it. It does not matter how it is organized. It does not matter how cute its labels are. All that matters is whether the kids can find books they can read and want to read. Does your classroom library meet the reading needs and interests of the kids in this room right now?

Teachers fret about organizational systems and other management aspects of their classroom libraries. We understand that keeping track of books and successfully housing books on shelves until you can get them to readers presents a lot of challenges for teachers. We have been there. We do not profess to have the perfect solutions to your organizational demands. What we have learned is that kids almost always show us the way to what they need if we pay attention and listen. Responding to kids' needs and shifting the classroom library when necessary (and possible) will guide you to develop an organizational plan that works for you.

The two of us have found it useful to talk with lots of other teachers about their classroom organizational systems, their thinking behind those systems, and how kids lead them to make decisions about their classroom libraries.

For this book, we were able to chat with experienced teachers who have curated classroom libraries for their students. We asked them to share with us how they organized their classroom libraries and why.

Organizing Your Classroom Library

Katherine Sokolowski, Lynsey Burkins, and Franki Sibberson

Comparing Middle School and Elementary School

Katherine Sokolowski, seventh-grade English teacher, Monticello, Illinois

Colby: Katherine, why don't you just tell us a little bit about your classroom library?

Katherine: My classroom library has evolved over the 26 years that I have been in education. When I started in elementary school, it was in the corner of my classroom. It was not very organized in any way. I eventually decided that I wanted the classroom library to circle the room, so I added shelves and moved books. The books were in baskets and organized alphabetically (by author). The library has evolved again. My middle school students asked me to take the books out of the baskets. Now, we have them on the shelves, organized by genre.

Now that I am teaching middle school, the reading levels of the classroom library books range from picture books through high school YA books. The two main parts of the room are nonfiction and fiction, but each part is broken down into smaller genres. The kids have a lot of say in the classroom library and how it works for them, what books are missing, and where the gaps (in our collection) are. The other big piece of it is that—as you know—the library has to be weeded. Often, this is the hardest thing for me to do! Sometimes, there are books that I can easily see need to go, but sometimes I have favorites that have not connected with students over time. When that happens, it is time for me to let those books go.

Co-Teaching With a Classroom Library

Lynsey Burkins, third-grade teacher, Dublin, Ohio

Colby: Lynsey, can you talk about how your classroom library is organized?

Lynsey: I have struggled with the idea held by some teachers who say, "I let the kids organize the classroom library," or "I think it's important that the kids do it." I want my students to have agency. I teach them toward independence. I teach them toward self-discovery and helping. But not the classroom library. I don't hold tight to much, but I do hold tight to the classroom library organization. I have gotten some pushback from colleagues about my stance, but I am finally comfortable in my own skin. Listen, if I know that books save lives, I know the power of the classroom library will affect every aspect of the school day—whether reading, writing, social studies, social and emotional learning, science—all day long. There's a book from the classroom library involved. There are instructional decisions that come from books we read from that library.

My most powerful co-teacher is the classroom library, and I need a literacy expert. I try to construct a space that invites kids to enter with the most freedom they can. The organization is pretty basic. The classroom library is not one spot in the classroom—it's around the room. There's a space for biographies, poetry, and fiction. Fiction is broken into two spaces—a section for books with more fantastical characteristics like talking animals, and another section that includes fictional books about people. There's a section for series books, too.

I have two large bookshelves on wheels for the informational books. It's easy to wheel them around while I am conferring and working with kids. Kids can go straight into browsing, and I want them to browse. The shelf labels for the classroom library are kids' book recommendations and photographs. At the beginning of the year, the shelves are unlabeled, but as kids find books and read them, we add their photos to the shelves carrying their favorite books.

Donalyn: What about graphic novels? Do you have your graphic novels spread through all of your books? Or do they have a section of their own?

Lynsey: I played with that. Now, I have graphic novels in our informational section because they're informational. In the series books, you'll find graphic novels series. There are some graphic picture books that are in the picture book section. I guess they're spread out!

Donalyn: This just reminds us that "graphic novel" describes a format and not a genre. Readers are going to find them in every genre. Colby, didn't you take your graphic novels and spread them into the genre sections one time? It didn't go well?

Colby: Barnes & Noble tried to do the same thing. But then they noticed they weren't selling as many copies of Raina Telgemeier's *Smile* and Kazu Kibuishi's *Amulet* (and other books) because no one could find them.

Lynsey: One year, I tried not to even delineate between a chapter book and picture book. Then, kids were asking for the series. I tried to move the informational alongside the fiction. I have tried it all. Right now, the organizational system we have is working.

Donalyn: Here's the thing—your kids *are* organizing the classroom library—just like Colby's kids. You have created the perfect partnership between the experienced literacy educator in the room, and the children and their expertise as readers. You are kidwatching and tweaking the library in response to what your students show you they want and need. If the kids aren't organizing the library, who is?

Colby: It is evident, Lynsey, and we share your belief, that there is not a specific way to organize your classroom library or label your bins. Your system makes sense. How much sense it makes to your kids is important. No classroom library will be exactly like yours. It's not a classroom library in a box—not just with the books, but also the organization and design.

Lynsey: Don't you think that the layout of your classroom really also dictates how you set it up?

Donalyn: You have space limitations.

Lynsey: You really do. So, I think your space and how you want the kids to move about that space also dictates what the classroom library might look like.

Organizing the Classroom Library in Response to Kids' Development and Interests

Franki Sibberson, former fifth-grade teacher, Dublin, Ohio

Colby: It's tricky. In elementary school, our classroom is our reading workshop space, but it is also our math workshop space. It is also our science room. Franki, how about you? Can you tell us about the organizational journey of your library?

Franki: When I read *The Third Teacher: 79 Ways You Can Use Design to Transform Teaching and Learning*, I realized how the classroom environment teaches. So, I know that the classroom library can teach kids. For example, when I taught kindergarten, I realized that my students didn't know what an author was, but if I put a picture of the author on their basket of books, kids would learn who an author was.

In my experience, how the classroom library is stocked and organized depends on which grade I'm teaching. In third grade, it was the series baskets. I wanted kids to find a character they loved and discover other series to read. In fifth grade, my students were still into reading series, but they would also fall in love with an author or genre. So, I changed the library a bit in response, supporting them toward independence. I really believe the library teaches kids about books by the way it is set up. So, I set up the classroom library by thinking about what my students might learn. Then, based on what I observe, I will rearrange it.

Colby: Can you give us an example?

Franki: The last year I taught fifth grade, reading novels in verse was suddenly a huge thing. I had a large group of kids that liked to read novels in verse, and some kids realized they liked historical fiction. So we created spaces in the classroom library for those types of books. They just grew and grew. I told the kids, "Hey! Whoever likes novels in verse, if you have a recommendation, throw it in this basket," or "I see a lot of you like historical fiction! Let's start pulling some." So, that section grows naturally. It wasn't like those books were hard to find the way that I had it organized. That wasn't the point. It's about paying attention to what a group of students shows interest in reading and what they start talking about. Then you make space in the classroom library for them to share.

As Franki, Lynsey, and Katherine shared, classroom libraries shift in response to students' needs and the teacher's increasing understanding of books and how to use a classroom library to engage kids with reading. In the next section, Colby explains how his collection—and his attitude toward it—has changed over the years.

COLBY'S CLASSROOM

Organization Changes Over Time

When I began building my classroom library, I was mostly focused on increasing the quantity of books. I'd beg parents to send in books during spring cleaning, pick up books at garage sales and Goodwill, and spend any extra cash I could scrounge to buy discounted titles on eBay. During that time, I was never worried about running out of space. My classroom library began as just a couple of built-in shelves under a window in my classroom. All the books were crammed together on the shelf. There was no organization—just a few dozen books.

The collection slowly grew, and I realized that kids were having a really hard time finding books. Donalyn's *The Book Whisperer* helped me organize my classroom library based on genre to help kids find books that they wanted to read, based on their reading preferences. I purchased a dozen or so plastic boxes from the local grocery store and started some genre tubs. I started with the genres Donalyn described, then began to revise them based on the needs of my students. I realized that I didn't need tubs for traditional literature or science fiction (two genres Donalyn used with her older students in Texas), but graphic novels were starting to explode with my readers, so I started a tub for them.

The change to organized tubs seemed to really help kids find books they wanted to read, and it also helped me quickly find a specific book I wanted to recommend to a reader.

The collection started to grow, and the one tub of realistic fiction books grew to four, then five, then six. When I was looking for a particular book, such as Barbara O'Connor's *How to Steal a Dog*, I couldn't find it. I had to go through all the realistic fiction tubs and hope I'd see it. Kids were also getting frustrated. They were spending valuable reading time trying to find a specific book that they wanted to read. At this point, I divided the realistic fiction into smaller sections. I had tubs with ranges of letters for authors' last names: A–L, M–R, and S–Z. These smaller sections helped because the kids and I had fewer tubs to dig through. We could narrow a range, at least. Now, when I looked for *How to Steal a Dog*, I only looked through one or two M–R tubs before I found it.

Moving to Third Grade

When I moved districts and grades—from fourth to third—it was the first time I seriously weeded my classroom library. I had to leave behind all the books that my former district had purchased. I also wanted to leave behind some books that I felt were better suited for a fourth-grade classroom. Whoever took my position would have at least a few books to start. The thought of removing books from my classroom library circulation never crossed my mind.

That summer, I had a lot of fun investigating chapter book series that I thought would be a good fit for my new third graders. Assuming that these younger readers would be into series when the year started, I pulled books from the genre tubs and created more series tubs for books I thought my students might enjoy, such as Geronimo Stilton, Junie B. Jones, and The Magic Tree House. These were series that other third-grade teachers recommended to me. I also created more author tubs during this time. No more running from fantasy to realistic fiction, searching for a few Kate DiCamillo books to share with a reader because they loved *Because of Winn-Dixie*. All of DiCamillo's books were nestled together in their own tub.

During this summer transition, I realized that my classroom in the new district didn't have the built-in bookshelves that I had in my former classroom. I convinced my father and uncle-in-law to help me build bookshelves. We measured around the room and designed shelves to fit the space. We built one set of shelves that would fit right under the whiteboard, and another set of shelves that were a little taller. These could line any walls that didn't have built-in bookshelves.

Moving to Fifth Grade

During my four years of teaching third grade, my library continued to grow. It was about to explode when I learned that I would be moving to fifth grade the following year. This move helped me avoid having to make tough choices about weeding books. The thought of getting rid of books still seemed a little out there to me.

I left a lot of books behind for the new third-grade teacher, moved my family-built bookshelves, and packed up my library. At the end of that summer, I got a text from my principal, Ms. Haney, asking me whether I needed any new bookshelves. Of course I did! A local university was tearing down an old dormitory, and they told us that we could take any furniture that we wanted. For the next several days, we loaded up my car and Ms. Haney's car, and even my dad came by with his truck for a couple of loads. We brought over enough bookshelves for several of our teachers to use for their classroom libraries. These bookshelves were pretty high quality, so I was able to get rid of a few of the garage-sale specials I had collected.

Within a year of teaching fifth grade, the classroom library had ballooned to more than 2,500 books. The graphic novel section alone was nearing 500 titles. I finally accepted that I really needed to weed books. Focusing on adding books that kids wanted to read and getting rid of the books they weren't reading made a huge difference. Kids were not wasting as much time digging through books no one wanted to read.

One summer, I talked with my friend Margie Culver, a retired school librarian, about how my kids could never find nonfiction books they wanted to read. She helped me understand that the nonfiction sections of our classroom library needed to be broken down into more specific topics. Having 12 tubs labeled "Animals" doesn't help a horse-loving reader find a stack of books about their favorite topic. Margie and I spent days breaking down the nonfiction books into topics that are much more user-friendly.

Each summer, I try to tweak things to help make the library more user-friendly for my readers. While it is hard to let go of books sometimes, I know that the most important thing is fine-tuning the classroom library so that readers have the best chance for reading success.

The best system is one you can maintain when your students arrive. Organizing the classroom library doesn't require a particular system, and you will frequently modify how you organize the books in response to your students and your evolving collection. Along with methods for organizing books and shelves, many teachers desire a system for checking out the classroom library books. In our experiences, checkout systems have some advantages and drawbacks.

Checking Out Books

Managing a classroom library collection requires teachers to keep track of their books somehow. With kids constantly checking out books from the collection and taking them out of your classroom, it can be challenging to get books returned. The two of us can relate to your frustration when Book One in a popular series remains checked out all year or that new book you just added to the library is already missing. Like you, we just don't want to lose all our classroom library books! The two of us have tried many types of book inventory checkout systems, with mixed results. No matter how simple or useful a checkout system might be, it becomes an instant failure when kids cannot use it consistently or easily.

Buy a self-inking stamp with your name on it, and stamp all of your books on the inside cover or title page and on the outside edge of the pages. Some teachers use a permanent marker or duct-tape labels. Invite your class librarians or a volunteer to stamp your books. This will bring more of your missing books back to you than anything else!

Donalyn had some success keeping track of books by taking photos of students holding books they were checking out. These "shelfies" stayed on the photo roll of the device until the book was returned.

The Best Checkout System May Be No System at All

Ultimately, the two of us have found that the honor system (take as many books as you want and bring them back when you are done), encouraging our students to take ownership of the classroom library, and getting students to track down missing books for us worked better than any checkout system. Yes, you will lose books when you stop using a system. You were losing books when you were using that system, too, weren't you?

In the words of a famous blonde cartoon princess, "Let it go."

While we would never recommend that teachers let their classroom books walk out the door, we have found that most systems do not work effectively for the entire school year without putting substantial work on the teacher and control on students. This makes most checkout systems unsustainable— no matter how well-designed or intentioned. As scary as it seems, jettisoning our classroom library checkout systems benefited our students and us in ways we could not predict. And we did not lose substantially more books than we did the years we chased kids down for every book.

Some Benefits of an Honor System

An honor system is less stressful and time-consuming. Keeping up a classroom library takes a lot of work. If your classroom library checkout system takes up a lot of time or involves a lot of monitoring, what could you be doing instead? Conferring with students or helping them find books? Going home earlier?

Checkout systems reinforce to kids that the books belong to the school instead of the students. Kids will better maintain the collection when they feel ownership for the books and understand that the resource is valuable to readers.

The absence of a formal system streamlines book borrowing. When kids have to check out every book you hand them or a friend hands them, the natural process of exchanging books slows down. Kids may be less likely to take a book from a peer if they must take time to check it out.

Colby has seen firsthand how restrictions have prevented his students from sharing books with each other or checking them out. Quarantining books during the pandemic impeded the natural exchanges of books between readers in his class. Reflecting on how a safety practice like the "quarantine box" changed the reading culture in his classroom, Colby continuously reflects on how rules and policies such as this one can become barriers to students' book access and impede free flowing conversations about books between his students.

The Quarantine Box

During much of the 2020–2021 school year, like many schools throughout the country, we quarantined books when kids were done reading them. We had to quarantine books for 48 hours. That meant that if a kid turned in a book at the end of the day on Tuesday, I wouldn't be able to get it back into the classroom library until Friday. Any book turned in on Thursday or Friday wouldn't be available to readers until the following Monday. When Dav Pilkey's new series, Cat Kid Comic Club, was released in the beginning of December, my fifth graders were excited to read it. My preorder was sitting on my doorstep when I got home that day, and I excitedly brought it to school Wednesday. The first kid that read the book finished it that night and returned it the next morning. Since the next morning was a Thursday, that in-demand book sat in our quarantine box until Monday. The kids were so frustrated.

Passing Books From Kid to Kid

I didn't realize how many books get passed from kid to kid without ever making it back into our classroom library until this school year, when we were no longer quarantining books. Early in the year, I book-talked Megan E. Freeman's *Alone*. One of my fifth graders asked to read it. They loved it. Instead of returning the book to the classroom library, they handed it to a friend.

A couple of months later, I realized that *Alone* still hadn't made it back to the classroom library because it was being handed from kid to kid. Boston was the fifth grader reading it at this point. I asked her whether she knew anyone else who wanted to read it when she was done. She informed me that there was a list of readers in line to read the book and that she would be giving it to Maddie when she was done reading it. I, of course, asked to see the list, and she replied, "You can't see the list, Mr. Sharp. We keep it in our heads." They keep it in their heads. I didn't really know what to make of that statement, but it sounded to me like my readers were taking steps toward independence. If we had a more rigid checkout system in our classroom library, things like the "*Alone* list" might not have happened. As much as I love having a lot of books in my classroom library, the dream is for those books to instead find their way into the hands and hearts of readers.

Building a classroom library collection is a career-long work in progress that evolves and changes in response to students. Before the school year begins, you have predicted some potential needs based on your past experiences and book knowledge. You've acquired a few books, developed some evaluation and weeding skills, and organized the shelves, bins, and books as best you can. You've set the stage for reading engagement, but students will be the final judge on whether your classroom library piques their interest and influences their reading volume and variety (Harvey, Ward, Hoddinott, & Carroll, 2021). In the next chapter, we will share ideas for introducing students to the classroom library and launching a year of reading in your room.

TIME TO REFLECT

- **Work with a colleague to MUSTIE one section of your classroom library, such as one bookcase or one genre.** What sorts of books did you remove? What books were you reluctant to part with? Why? What surprised you about the books you weeded? Partner with a grade-level colleague and help each other weed. What did your colleague notice about the books in your library that you missed?

- **Now, use one of the culturally responsive evaluation resources we recommended on page 39, such as Teaching for Change's Guide to Selecting Anti-Bias Children's Books.** What did you discover about the representation in your classroom library? What gaps do you see in your collection now? Whose voices are missing? How have your weeding and evaluation activities influenced your priorities for text selection? What are your priorities now, and why?

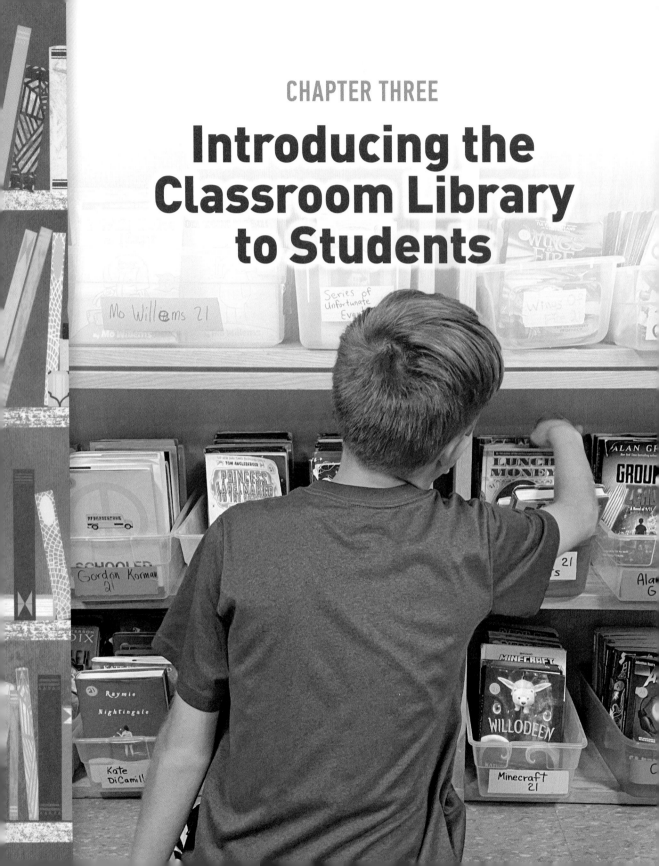

CHAPTER THREE

Introducing the Classroom Library to Students

Reimagining and rearranging your classroom library can help you match students with books and encourage them to read. But until students arrive, you cannot predict all their needs and interests. Your new students' experience with previewing and self-selecting books will vary, and they will need different degrees of modeling, instruction, and practice before feeling confident enough to use the classroom library. In the first few weeks, you can build a foundation for using the classroom library—and reading—all year.

Students use the library from the first day of school. Colby spends the beginning of the year setting up classroom rituals and routines for independent reading time, conferring, and read-alouds; teaching students the elements of various genres; and sharing many books. Colby dips into the classroom library as needed to select titles for instructional purposes, such as mini-lessons and read-alouds, or to find books for students to preview for independent reading.

Launching a Year of Reading:
The First Few Weeks of School

I spent the minutes before school making final touches on the classroom library—adding a couple of genre labels to book baskets, checking that the new graphic novel *Chunky* by Yehudi Mercado was displayed on top of the graphic novel bookshelf, and making sure that our first read-aloud, *Pax*, by Sara Pennypacker, was sitting on the whiteboard marker tray.

Waiting for the bell, I leafed through *Pax*. My heart pounded in anticipation. Would this class love graphic novels as much as my students in the past did? Which books would I need to add to the nonfiction section of our library once I got to know the interests of my kids? What impact would spending 15 months in virtual pandemic learning have on the reading lives of my new students?

When the bell rang, I stood in the hallway to greet my new students. Kids entered the room, found their seats, and waited for me to give them direction. Once most of the kids had entered the room, I joined them. Many of them were chatting with their classmates and looked happy to be back in school. A few kids were gathered in the classroom library. I noticed that they were holding a book, so I made my way over to see which book had caught their attention. "Mr. Sharp, check out this book we found in the classroom," Wyatt said. They were holding *The Cursed Castle: An Escape Room in a Book* by L. J. Tracosas.

"Cool! Do you like books like this?" I asked. They all nodded before going back to looking at the ghost stories in the book together. What other mysteries might they like? I told them we were going to study a big historical mystery—the Roanoke Colony—in Social Studies soon.

Connecting With the First Read-Aloud

When it was time to introduce kids to our first read-aloud and the classroom library, I told them about how I fell in love with reading in the classroom next door. When I was nine years old, my teacher, Mrs. Collins, and our student teacher, Mr. Bongtrager, read aloud Gary Paulsen's

Hatchet to my fourth-grade classroom. "Mr. Greenslade read our class *Hatchet*," Jovelle said. Kids throughout the room nodded their approval. I smiled as I walked to the back of the classroom. I showed kids the section of our classroom library that was organized by authors I had learned fifth graders tend to really like—Kwame Alexander, Kate Messner, and Katherine Applegate.

I asked the class to share their favorite books that their teachers had read aloud to them during their time in school. "*The Wild Robot!*" one of my fifth graders called out. "Oh yeah! That one was awesome," another kid said. Letting the kids talk about their love for Peter Brown's *The Wild Robot* and *The Wild Robot Returns*, I moved to the front of the classroom and stood next to the fantasy section of our classroom library. When the conversation quieted down, I showed kids where they could find *The Wild Robot* if they wanted to read it.

"Mr. Greenslade also read *Bud, Not Buddy*," Wyatte shared. I moved to the historical fiction section of our library and showed kids our classroom copy of Christopher Paul Curtis's beloved classic. I asked, "Have you heard of the companion novel, *The Mighty Miss Malone?*' They shook their heads no. Their confused looks told me that I needed to teach them about the difference between books in a series and companion books.

After the conversation about favorite read-alouds died down, I introduced the class to our first read-aloud, *Pax*. I showed them the cover of the book. They shared their observations. "Looks like the title might be the name of the animal on the front." "I think that is a fox." "I hope it doesn't die." "I wonder if the animal talks." I told the class that the book is about a boy and his pet fox. Then I explained that the chapters alternate between the boy's story and the fox's story. I asked, "Has anyone else read a book like that?" One of the kids mentioned R. J. Palacio's *Wonder*. The kids seemed excited to get started, so I opened the book and began to read.

Everyone Chooses a Book

After a couple of chapters of *Pax*, I told students that it was time for them to pick a book to read. They could read a book they brought from home, or they could select one from our classroom library. I told them that I was setting a mental timer for five minutes, and that I would love for them to all have a book to read once that timer went off.

The kids quickly dispersed around the room. A handful checked out the Gary Paulsen book tub and other books organized by authors, about half the class congregated around the graphic novel section, and the rest explored the books organized by genres. None of my students went to the nonfiction section of the library. I made a mental note to book-talk some nonfiction books in the coming days to help my readers discover the nonfiction section of our library.

I could see how caught up in the excitement and clearly engaged the students were, so I gave them a few extra minutes. When they finished browsing, all my students had selected a book and returned to their seats.

I passed out a stack of sticky notes to each table group and asked students to write down the reason they selected their book. As they finished their notes, kids stuck them on the whiteboard at the front of our classroom. Kids read their books until everyone finished.

Once all the notes trickled in, I brought the class together and began reading the sticky notes aloud. Some highlights:

- Squish is a good series and similar to Babymouse.
- It looks cool.
- I picked *The One and Only Bob* because I love animal books, and I liked both the book and the movie *The One and Only Ivan*.
- Because it is scary, and I like scary books.
- Teacher gave it to me.

While I read their notes out loud, I began organizing them by topic. I placed them in six different categories. Next, I reread the sticky notes from each section and asked students to consider what each section of notes had in common. By the end of our conversation, we had identified six ways readers select books:

1. Series: Students gravitate toward series, and the buzz around series can forge relationships between readers in a classroom. Series are a great way for kids to build reading momentum and make reading plans because they do not have to consider what they might read next or search for another book—the series provides a plan.

2. Author: By the time kids meet me in fifth grade, they know that if they love a book by an author, chances are they might love another book by that same author. Identifying authors that they love is a great way for kids to strengthen their understanding of their reading identity. They recognize more about their own preferences when they can name a few favorite authors.

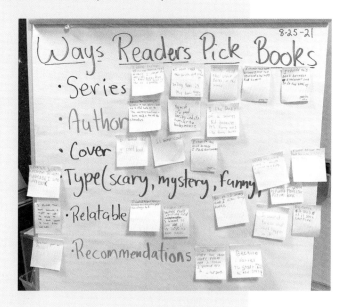

3. Cover: Yes, we judge books by their covers. It is often the first thing that we see, and there is no shame in trying a book because the cover is visually appealing. After all, publishers design covers to attract readers!

4. Type (horror, humor, mystery, etc.): Just as we have preferences for the types of movies and TV shows we like to watch, we have preferences for the types of books we like to read, and it's no different for kids. Kids who are binge-watching *Stranger Things* are often the same kids that can't get enough of K. R. Alexander's books, for example. Both stories are creepy and scary!

5. Relatability: As we discussed reasons for why kids chose a book, they often made connections to themselves: the character has braces like I do. I picked it because I'm allergic to pets like the character. Or, I have a brother and two sisters just like the main character.

6. Recommendations: When someone you trust in your reading community recommends a book to you, it makes you want to learn more about the book. Recommending books to each other is something that we will do daily for the entire school year, so I loved seeing students doing it at the beginning of the year.

Obviously, these are not all the reasons that readers select books, but it was a great start to a list that we would end up referring to throughout the first semester of the school year.

Moving Into Independent Reading and Reading Aloud

From this conversation, my students moved to their first experience with independent reading in their new classroom. While they read, I was tempted to bounce around and start conferring with my readers. Instead, I gave them space to read. I found a comfortable spot in the classroom and read with them.

We ended our first day—like we would end just about every school day—with a picture book read-aloud. We read Adam Rex's and Christian Robinson's *School's First Day of School*. I love reading this book to kids early in the school year because I think kids entering a new classroom community can often feel like the school felt in this book—nervous, unsure of what to expect, and in the end, hopeful for what the year has to offer. I also like to refer back to the book when we talk about the fantasy genre on Day Two. The kids can identify this book as fantasy because the school is a character who thinks and talks. The kids seemed to love the story. They laughed, smiled, and pointed to things in the illustrations they noticed. Day One was in the books. I felt good about being back in the classroom library with kids, which helped set the tone for the year. We are going to be surrounded by books. Books are part of what we do. After a year of being separated from the books and from each other, I was grateful and energized.

Shortly after school ended, our superintendent emailed us that the last two days of the week were moving from full days to half days because of the extreme heat. Our classrooms are not air-conditioned and have been known to reach 90+ degrees on hot afternoons. I welcomed the relief from the heat, but my lesson plans had just taken a massive hit. Teachers can relate!

My goals for the second day of school were to read aloud *Pax*, give kids time to read independently, and introduce our first genre—fantasy. The read-aloud and independent reading both went smoothly. Kids seemed to enjoy *Pax* and Peter's journey, and they were settling into their independent reading books.

Introducing Genres and Reading Aloud

To introduce kids to the various genres in our classroom library, I follow this routine:

- Read a picture book from each genre.
- Discuss with students their observations about that genre.
- Create an anchor chart of qualities for that genre.
- Move on to another genre and repeat.

To introduce students to fantasy, I read Dan Santat's Caldecott Medal-winning book *The Adventures of Beekle: The Unimaginary Friend*. Our anchor chart included everyone's observations of what we can expect from the literary elements in fantasy books: characters, plot, and setting. You could leave a space at the bottom of the anchor chart to include examples where kids are able to share any fantasy books they had read.

On Day Three we examined realistic fiction through the lens of Dan Yaccarino's *The Longest Storm*. Day Four, we looked at our first biography, *Shirley Chisholm Dared* by Alicia D. Williams and April Harrison. With each new genre, the kids were able to talk about the similarities and differences they saw between the books, and they started to identify things they liked about each genre.

Setting Up Reading Binders

Starting the year with three half days, it took until the second week of school to set up our reading binders. Our binders are divided into different sections. The sheets we use in our binders came from Donalyn's *Reading in the Wild* (2013), and I've made some minor tweaks here and there to meet the needs of the readers I have in front of me. These sheets include spaces for students to record the books they plan to read or finish reading:

To-Read List: At the beginning of the year, students' to-read lists were a three-column table, with the headers "Title," "Author," and "Read." The Read column gives kids a place to check off any books they eventually read. Often, kids mark off books they previously recorded on their to-read lists because they decide later that they don't want to read them anymore.

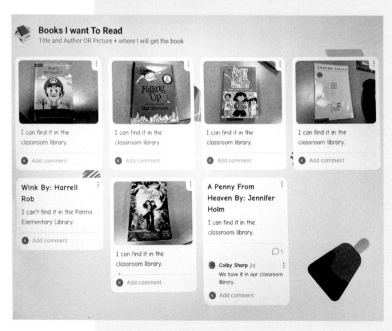

Midway through the school year, I had students transfer their to-read lists to a Padlet wall. Padlet, an iPad app, allowed my students to take pictures of the books that they wanted to read and add them to the pad. I noticed during reading conferences that many kids struggled to remember some of the books they had added to their to-read list during the school year. My hope was that the book-cover picture would help them recall more about the book and why they wanted to read it. I also encouraged the kids to record where and how they could find the book, so they could locate it when they wanted to read it. If it was a classroom library book, they added the book basket number. They also listed ways they could get the book: from a friend's collection, school library, public library, home, Target, bookstore, and so on.

This move to Padlet was intended to not only help kids quickly access the books they wanted to read, but to gradually move them away from solely relying on our classroom library for books. I wanted them to consider where else they could go in the future. At the end of the school year, they were all going to leave my classroom, and I didn't want any of them to lose their ability to get their hands on the books they wanted to read. An additional perk that I didn't think of when we moved to Padlet was the option for students to instantly share their to-read lists with classmates and me. I often check out their lists from my own iPad and leave comments on some of the books they have on their to-read wall. For example, I noticed recently that Kaelyn had Jennifer L. Holm's *Penny From Heaven* on her list. I commented, letting her know that I thought she would love the book and where she could find it in our classroom library.

Genre Graph: This bar graph is probably the sheet my students enjoy filling out the most. The X-axis of the graph lists the genres our library is divided into, and the Y-axis is the number of books read. When kids finish a book, they color in a rectangle on the graph above the genre of that book. They love seeing their progress grow throughout the year, and it is a quick way for them to be able to notice their reading preferences, as well as genres of books that they still might want to try.

Reading List: On these sheets, students keep a running list of the books they read throughout the year. When they start a book, they fill out the title, author, and genre and answer this question: "Why did I pick this book?" When students finish a book, they record the date and rank the book between one and five stars. If they choose to abandon the book, they just write the letter A in that box for "Abandoned."

I find kids' reading lists to be helpful when conferring with them. Understanding the ways they find books, how long it takes them to finish one, the percentage of books they abandon, and the genres that they are reading helps me celebrate their successes and work with them to set independent reading goals.

Status of the Class: I have managed the status of the class a bunch of different ways over the years. My school is a one-to-one iPad school, so I thought it would be cool to try using Padlet for status of the class this year. I created a Padlet wall organized into columns. Each student has a column. Every day, they update me about which book they are currently reading and what page they left off reading the day before—at school or home. If they start a new book, they are expected to share a cover image of it. If they abandon a book, they can share why it didn't work out. All of these brief, easy activities help me get to know them better as readers, give me teaching ideas for whole-group and one-on-one conferences, and help kids set goals for themselves.

After our first days together, I had already learned a lot about my students as readers:

- They were drawn to familiar and beloved series, such as Dog Man and Diary of a Wimpy Kid.

- Their knowledge about authors was limited to authors that were read aloud in fourth grade and the authors of the most popular graphic novel series.

- They had no interest in reading biographies, informational texts, or poetry. Zero. Zip. Nada.

- Most, if not all, had a positive attitude and genuine excitement toward reading.

By the end of the second week of school, Colby's students experience daily read-alouds and independent reading time. They understand the class routines, which Colby assembles for them in their reading binders. They have begun to build their knowledge of the characteristics of different genres. Students also freely explore and check out books from the classroom library, developing the confidence to use the library along the way.

In the first few weeks, Colby is able to identify some areas to address that can help his students grow as readers—their disinterest in certain genres and their narrow knowledge of authors and series, for example. Those observations will inform his future whole-class lessons and the texts he chooses to book-talk and read aloud.

> The more information we teachers acquire about our students as people and readers, the more effectively we can nurture them and support their developing reading identities.

Getting to Know Students as Readers

The more information we acquire about students as people and readers, the more effectively we can nurture them and support their developing reading identities. While every conversation with students provides insight as you listen and watch their behaviors, there are more formal ways to collect information about their interests and attitudes about reading, such as a survey administered during the first few days of the school year.

The Elementary Reading Attitude Survey—or "Garfield Survey"—(McKenna & Kear, 1990) allows you to capture students' responses to questions about their reading interests and behaviors at school and home. Students circle one of five Garfield the Cat images that range from happy to unhappy. The survey is easy to administer and evaluate and is backed by studies we trust that prove it to be a valid instrument. Colby's observations of his students' Garfield Survey responses show some similarities among students' impressions of reading for fun.

Evaluating Garfield Surveys

Reading through the Elementary Reading Attitude Survey, I noticed some common themes:

- Most kids felt positive about reading at school. More than half of the kids gave positive responses when asked about how they felt about reading at home for fun. I found it interesting that only three of my students had a more positive opinion of reading at home than school. This felt like a red flag that I wanted to explore more.

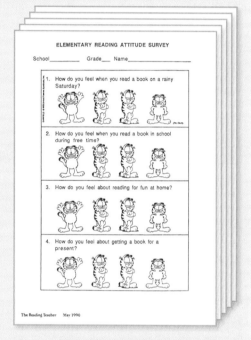

- The survey showed me that the kids did not have positive experiences with reading over the summer. I would support them to become habitual readers during the school year, so that they'd come to see reading as personally important and not just a school activity. If they read because they loved it and found value in it, I knew from experience they would read more next summer.

- Nearly all my fifth graders gave low marks to any questions about taking reading tests or completing reading worksheets. No surprises there, but it did send a signal to me that I had to earn their trust. Many had negative reading experiences connected to reading at school. I could show them that during our time together, my top priority during independent reading time would be to support them in reading the books they wanted.

Everyday Routines and Rituals

As teachers who strive to support and nurture students' reading lives, while also teaching them what they need to become more proficient readers, we rely on a few instructional routines and classroom rituals to engage students in reading and support skill-building alongside whole-class and small-group instruction.

Time to Read

Kids need to read approximately 20–30 minutes every day from a wide range of texts and in a variety of contexts, including independent reading (Hiebert & Reutzel 2010; McFarland, et al., 2018). Providing students with daily time to read increases their motivation to read and allows you to evaluate their progress toward academic and personal reading goals. While kids read, you confer!

We start the year reading for 10 minutes a day and build up to at least 30 minutes a day. Some years we hit that goal in a month, and some years it takes closer to two.

Colby starts the year having his students read for 10 minutes a day and build up to at least 30 minutes a day.

Conferences

Meeting with students often to determine how they are developing as readers—in terms of their reading habits and their reading abilities—gives you opportunities to connect with students around their reading lives and scaffold their growing independence.

Our first reading conferences usually begin the third week of school. The first couple of weeks are spent helping the kids become independent: making sure they always have something to read, are filling out the forms in their reading notebook, and are selecting a place to read where distractions are limited.

Once the kids can read independently for 20–30 minutes, Colby begins one-on-one reading conferences. During the first couple of conferences, he and the student go over their responses to the reading attitude survey, and he talks to them about the positive and negative reading experiences they have had during their reading life.

Choice of Books

Students read more and enjoy reading more when they self-select books. Modeling, practice, and support in choosing their own books foster students' reading motivation and their confidence (Guthrie, Wigfield, & VonSecker, 2000; Reis et al., 2007; Tatum, 2009; Brooks & Frankel, 2019).

From day one, Colby's students know that the books they are going to read during independent reading will be books they choose. During the first couple of weeks, Colby also talks to his students about why it is important to try different types of books. Reading widely keeps our reading lives more interesting and can lead us to discover new favorites. By sharing his reading life with his students, Colby helps them to see the benefits of being a well-rounded reader.

Read-Alouds

Listening to a fluent reader remains one of the most effective ways to build children's background knowledge, vocabulary, and knowledge of text structure and story grammar. Read-alouds also create shared moments for connection within the class and offer opportunities for teachers to expand students' understanding of genres, formats, topics, and perspectives they might not read on their own. Those introductions support independent reading and inquiry.

When selecting books to read aloud to his students, Colby almost always keeps these two questions front of mind:

1 **How will this book lead to more reading?** Read-alouds are a great way to introduce kids to new authors, series, formats, and genres. Colby's hope is that by reading aloud Barbara O'Connor's *Wish*, a handful of kids in his class might realize they love realistic fiction, or that they want to explore other titles by O'Connor.

2 **Is this a book that at least one reader will remember for the rest of their life?** We believe that reading aloud is one of the best ways to help kids fall in love with reading, and for many kids it just takes one book to light that flame. The books that Colby chooses to read aloud have the power to get the fire started.

While the daily activities in our classrooms may shift from one day to the next, by dedicating time for students to read, encouraging their choices, reading aloud (at least once a day), and conferring with students as often as possible, we are able to support our readers while also managing our other instructional demands. The classroom library and school library serve as the primary sources for books and reading material for these activities. For students to capitalize on abundant book access, though, many of them need to increase their knowledge of the books available for them to read and learn how to evaluate them.

Building Students' Book Knowledge

According to the *Scholastic Kids & Family Reading Report* (2019), many young people feel that their parents and caregivers underestimate the difficulty of finding books to read. When kids read widely and voluminously, they accumulate reading experiences that inform future choices. They build a deeper understanding of the types of books available to them, expand their awareness of authors and illustrators, and develop individual preferences and tastes in reading material. The same report also revealed that the more kids read, the more confident they become in locating and choosing books for themselves.

To self-select books wisely, kids need lots of opportunities to preview, share, and talk about books they might read. Independent reading only benefits students when they can comprehend the books they have chosen to read. To determine that students are making adequate developmental progress, we teachers often center reading conferences on books students are currently reading or recently finished (or abandoned). We must determine whether students can understand what they read and commit to finishing books. Spend some time during conferences talking with students about their reading plans. Those who do not have a plan may benefit from your guidance and encouragement.

> When kids read widely and voluminously, they accumulate reading experiences that inform future choices.

How can we leverage our classroom libraries and daily literacy activities to expose students to more books they might read? It starts with access, which helps them navigate a collection and successfully use it.

As we explained, curating and organizing the classroom library with students in mind will create an enticing space. However, many students tell us that too many books can be intimidating. Where are the good books? Where do they start? It does not matter how thoughtful your classroom collection is if kids will not interact with it or lack confidence in choosing books from it. Let's tap into some tried-and-true practices that strengthen students' literacy development and their ability to choose books on their own.

Reading Aloud in the Primary Grades—and Beyond

Reading aloud is an influential practice for building reading and listening skills and engaging students. Listening to regular read-alouds positively influences literacy development, leading to increased fluency (Blau, 2001) and vocabulary acquisition (Beck & McKeown, 2000). Because read-aloud is traditionally viewed as a literacy activity for young children, many caregivers and teachers discontinue it when children's independent reading proficiency grows. By fourth grade, only 21 percent of parents and caregivers report regularly reading aloud to their children at least five days a week. By middle school, reading aloud at home falls to 7 percent.

Reading aloud at school doesn't fare much better. The peak year for students to experience frequent read-alouds at school is also fourth grade. After that, read-alouds at school drop off a cliff (Scholastic, 2019).

> Readers do not outgrow read-alouds. If they did, the audiobook market would not increase year after year.

Readers do not outgrow read-alouds. If they did, the audiobook market would not increase year after year (Faverio & Perrin, 2022). Reading aloud to middle school students with reading disabilities, including dyslexia, can help them (Shurr & Taber-Doughty, 2012). The benefits of read-alouds extend beyond language arts courses, too. Hurst and Griffity found that read-alouds in science class can improve students' attitudes about science, as well as their comprehension (2014).

Beyond the academic value of read-alouds, when teachers select read-alouds that capture a wide range of people and topics—particularly the stories and experiences of historically marginalized people—it can increase students' social comprehension (Ahmed, 2018) and compassion for others (Kidd & Castano, 2013) and may help counter prejudices and biases (Johnson, et al., 2014).

Colby's daily read-alouds quickly forge relationships between his students and give them guided opportunities to practice evaluating and discussing books. Students often extend their enjoyment for the read-aloud book by reading more books by the same author or exploring the topics introduced in the text. Let Origami Yoda show us the way. Colby's read-aloud of this book sparked a lot of interest among students.

Reading Aloud *The Strange Case of Origami Yoda*

My students and I gathered on the carpet to finish reading aloud Tom Angleberger's *The Strange Case of Origami Yoda*. The kids were eager to find out whether Tommy would ask Sarah to dance and to learn what her response might be. I had read this book aloud a handful of times, so I knew that I was going to have to deal with some tears slipping out of my eyes at the moment where Tommy decides that he would rather be on Dwight's side than Harvey's side. The kids had been rooting for Tommy to make the right decision—even though it was tough.

When we finished the book, the kids cheered. It ended the way most of them had hoped, and they were blown away by how so many of the events in the book came together. Before we left the carpet, Levi asked if he could go to the classroom library and borrow the next book in the series, *Darth Paper Strikes Back*. I nodded, and he skipped to the Tom Angleberger tub located in the author/series section of our classroom library.

The rest of the class went to their seats for independent reading time, and I grabbed my reading conference binder. Mason greeted me at my desk and said, "Um... Mr. Sharp, I'd like to borrow that Origami Yoda book. Would that be okay?" I handed him the book, and then I headed to my first reading conference of the afternoon.

A few minutes later, in a very quiet room filled with kids lost in their books, Levi said, "Oh no. Everything is all wrong. What is happening to these kids?" I smiled, knowing that he was in for an adventure with *Darth Paper Strikes Back*. The kids in the room looked up from their books for a moment. When they realized Levi had gone back to reading, they did the same.

The Force Is Strong...

The next day, Levi rushed into the room and slapped down *Darth Paper Strikes Back* on his desk. "It was so good, Mr. Sharp. I need to get *The Secret of the Fortune Wookie*," he said. I smiled as Levi headed to the library with that same skip in his step that he had the day before.

As more kids entered the room, I noticed that there was a gaggle of readers gathering around Levi's desk. I poked my head into the group to see what was going on. Levi not only read all of *Darth Paper Strikes Back* in a day, but he also found time to create a whole bunch of Star Wars origami characters. I pulled out my phone and ordered some origami paper for the class.

Star Wars origami characters that Levi created after reading *Darth Paper Strikes Back*.

In the coming days, Levi continued to make his way through the Origami Yoda series and fold lots of cool characters out of our new stack of origami paper. When I sat down to confer with him, he said to me, "Mr. Sharp, these books are changing my life. I've never minded reading, but these books are making me love it. They really did change my life." I smiled. Levi and I talked about some other books that he might be interested in trying after he finished the series.

In the back of the room, I noticed that Remmy was now reading *Darth Paper Strikes Back*. He was holding the book with one hand, and on the other he wore a pretty sick Origami Yoda finger puppet. I decided to divert from my plan for my next conference so that I could see how his journey with the series was going. Remmy and I talked about his finger puppet and his thoughts on *Darth Paper Strikes Back*. I was curious to know more about his choice. Remmy was usually reading something written by Gary Paulsen. Remmy admitted that he wasn't a very big Star Wars fan, but that he really liked the characters in *The Strange Case of Origami Yoda* and loved creating origami.

About two weeks after we finished our read-aloud of *The Strange Case of Origami Yoda*, we had all fallen in love with Melody, the main character in our new read-aloud *Out of My Mind* by Sharon Draper. When my kids headed back to their desks after the read-aloud to begin independent reading, Mason came up and handed me *Origami Yoda*. "Thanks for letting me borrow it," he said. "Last night I finished reading it aloud to my grandma. She really liked it. I think we might read *Darth Paper Strikes Back* together, too." I didn't really know what to say to that, so I just smiled and gave him a high five.

The Lasting Benefits of Reading Aloud

Colby's read-aloud of *The Strange Case of Origami Yoda* illustrates how students enjoyed the shared experience of reading the book. Beyond the read-aloud, this positive reading experience and students' awareness and appreciation for Tom Angleberger's series led them to more reading. How can read-alouds benefit students and construct a foundation for future classroom library use and more independent reading? While each read-aloud offers a unique experience, there are consistent benefits to reading aloud beyond the academic value:

Read-alouds expand students' book knowledge by introducing them to a variety of genres and formats, authors and illustrators, and voices and perspectives. As teachers, the two of us have been frustrated when our students pick the same books repeatedly or walk past engaging books in the classroom library. As we mentioned, many kids are overwhelmed and uncertain about what types of books are available for them to read. Through read-alouds, you show kids options for what they might read and increase their ability to self-select books. How can you use your read-aloud to show students more about how books are formatted and designed? How can you tap into students' interests when selecting read-alouds? How can you choose read-alouds that challenge students to read more widely?

Read-alouds send positive messages about reading. When the two of us talk with other adults about reading, do you know what their most positive memories of language arts class are to this day? The books, poems, and articles their teachers and librarians read to them. Think about it! For many of your students right now, their most powerful, joyful memories of your class might be your daily read-alouds. Learning to read is challenging, and kids need to see its value for them. If reading is always hard or always has academic strings, it is hard to keep kids excited about it.

Read-alouds foster community. The students in your classroom will show a range of reading abilities and enthusiasm. Because listening comprehension outpaces reading comprehension, read-alouds may offer the only opportunity in the school day for all of your students to engage in the same reading experience. No matter students' readiness, they can participate in the read-aloud experience. When we read aloud and engage in authentic discussion about the text, we model how readers consider and talk about books. These models support students' independent reading and writing (Varlas, 2018). Read-alouds provide more access for developing and emergent readers who may not be able to comprehend grade-level text, yet. Some students may require additional support, such as extra paper for doodling notes or a copy of the text to follow (Kluth and Chandler-Olcott, 2008).

In our teaching experiences, no instructional routine forges community more quickly than read-alouds do. No matter our students' reading experience or skills, they can discuss and share the read-aloud text. Read-alouds are the best part of the day!

Book Pass: Browsing and Previewing Classroom Library Books

Kids need lots of time and opportunities to look at books and consider reading them (Miller & Kelley, 2013). When readers have time to browse books, they build their knowledge of them and the variety of them. When kids preview, share, and discuss books to read, they are more likely to discover books they may enjoy. Talking about books with their peers strengthens reader-to-reader relationships, too.

Teachers and librarians can set aside time for students to look at many books and consider some for potential reading. Book passes, first developed by Janet Allen, offer a lively opportunity for students to examine books, preview them, and choose books for reading or adding to their to-read lists (Allen, 2000).

You can manage a book pass in various ways, but in general, select an assortment of books from your classroom library for kids to preview based on an upcoming unit or book club, or because you see a need with students' book choices—too many kids are avoiding the poetry section, for example. Students are given a short amount of time to preview books, then to reflect on whether they would like to read them or not. You can host a book-pass activity in your classroom or partner with your school library to hold a book pass in the library.

Host a book pass when:

- you introduce new books to the classroom library.
- students need to select a book for book clubs or genre study.
- students' choices are stale—reading the same books, going to the same sections of the library, and so on.
- students avoid or express dislike for certain genres or types of books.

Colby holds book passes throughout the year as a method for putting a lot of books in front of students that they might overlook, to feed students' preferences and interests by expanding their book knowledge, and to challenge students to read outside of their comfort zones.

A Book Pass Puts More Books in Front of Kids

While weeding a couple hundred books from the classroom library halfway through the school year, I kept noticing books that I thought my fifth graders would love to read—books that had been popular a few years ago, but that I hadn't seen any of my current students reading. When I saw Laurel Snyder's *Orphan Island*, I knew Kaelyn would love it. Erin Hagar's *The Inventors of LEGO® Toys* had Alex's name written all over it. We were at a point in the school year where most of my fifth graders were enjoying the book that they were reading, and they had three to five books on their to-read list. How could I get my students to look at these older books?

It was time for a book pass.

It felt like a book pass would also be a great way to introduce my students to some books they hadn't yet encountered and possibly to get their eyes on some books in genres they weren't reading much.

I decided to create five book-pass stations. For an earlier book pass, I had spread the books out so that each station had a variety of genres and formats. This time each station was more focused. I chose the stations based on my observations of students' preferences and the books they avoided reading.

Book Pass Stations

- **Fantasy:** A lot of my kids were reading and enjoying fantasy, so I thought it might be fun to introduce them to some of the fantasy books that hadn't been making the rounds.

- **Graphic Novels:** As with fantasy, graphic novels were very popular, but kids were only reading about 20 to 30 percent of the graphic novels in our classroom library. At this station, I placed a bunch of nonfiction titles from the Science Comics series, the first book in multiple graphic novels series, and other graphic novels that I was hoping the kids might add to their to-read list.

- **Biography:** Few of my readers had spent much time reading biographies, Just about anything I put at this station would be new to them. I selected a pile of high-interest picture book biographies, several biographies of athletes who might interest the kids, and a handful of books from the Who Was/Is? series.

- **Informational Text:** I had a lot of fun picking books for this one. This station included books about animals, space, dinosaurs, atlases, habitats, and more. I was eager to see how my students would respond to a station filled entirely with informational texts. Despite my efforts to book-talk nonfiction more and tinker with this section of the classroom library, kids weren't seeking out more informational texts to read.

- **Poetry:** While my students hadn't been reading as much poetry as I would have liked, this was one area of the classroom library that was starting to see increased traffic. Books such as Sharon Creech's *Love That Dog*, Megan E. Freeman's *Alone*, and Rajani LaRocca's *Red, White, and Whole* were finding their way into the hearts and hands of my readers. The goal of the station was to build on that momentum and encourage more poetry reading. This station was filled with poetry collections, novels in verse, and poetry picture books.

I explained each station to my students and told them they would have 12 minutes at each one. We discussed ways readers preview books and the benefits of adding books to our to-read lists. I asked them to share what they were hoping to get out of this activity. Zander said that he was excited to add some new graphic novels to his to-read list. I smiled. Zander had already read 32 picture books, and he was always looking for new ones to fall in love with. Jessica shared that she was interested in seeing what she would find at the biography station. Sophia was hoping to find a book like *Love That Dog* in the poetry section.

The kids grabbed their iPads so they could add books to their Padlet to-read lists. I told them they could take a book or two with them to the next station if they found one that they really wanted to read.

While the kids were busy with the first rotation, I found myself talking to Levi at the nonfiction station. He was looking at Steve Jenkins's *Dinosaurs by the Numbers*. He went on and on about how much he used to love reading dinosaur books. I asked him why he stopped reading them. He thought about it for a minute before saying, "I'm not sure, but I'm going to start reading them again today."

During one of the rotations, I was hanging out at the fantasy station when I saw Kent book-talk a title in the Rider Woofson series. He shared with his group mates how much he loved the book and encouraged them to give it a shot. A few kids added it to their to-read list.

One thing that I didn't expect during the book pass was how many kids would head to the classroom library to find books they remembered. When Daltin saw a classmate looking at Jerry Craft's *The New Kid*, he went to the library to grab Craft's *Class Act* for them. Another kid went to the classroom library to find Sharon Creech's *Hate That Cat*. He didn't book-talk it to anyone; instead he placed it at that station for other kids to discover.

The book pass was a huge success. When we debriefed at the end, every fifth grader had added multiple books to their to-read list. For the first time this school year, the class seemed excited to read biographies, poetry, and informational books.

The next day, I was conferring with Danny. He mentioned how much he had enjoyed the Steve Jenkins books that we read as a class a couple of weeks ago, and he was interested in reading some of Steve's infographic books from the book pass. We logged into my public library account and placed holds on a dozen of Jenkins's books. I could pick them up for Danny in the coming days.

There are times where we need to weed books from our classroom library when kids no longer seem interested in them, but there are also times where we need to carve out time for kids to explore some of the books that they haven't been reading. It is so easy to get into a groove with a genre, author, or series that we are super into reading. Taking time to explore fresh books can be a great way for kids to find books they might want to read or discover a new type of book that they love to read.

Book passes can reinvigorate kids' reading tastes by exposing them to books they might enjoy reading and expanding their book knowledge. They, along with book cafés, "speed dating" with books, and other previewing activities, can reveal the strategies students use to examine and select books and support your efforts to challenge students to read widely across genres, authors, and topics.

Preview Stacks: Browsing and Previewing Classroom Library Books

While the book-pass activity works best with the whole class, preview stacks provide individual opportunities to confer with young readers, determine their book selection strategies and reading tastes, and connect them with books they might read. As explained in *Reading in the Wild* (2013), teachers and librarians take their knowledge of books and of a particular reader and make a match. You collect four or five books of interest with a student in mind, then share the books with the student—giving the child time to preview the books and select one with support from you. For many kids, the ability to choose books freely in a large collection is more intimidating than enticing. They may lack effective strategies for previewing and evaluating books. They may need more support for finding books they can read about topics that interest them. Narrowing potential book choices to more personalized options scaffolds students' growing book selection skills and expands their book knowledge.

At the beginning of the year, fill preview stacks with titles of broad interest to kids in the grade you teach, such as the first books in popular series or evergreen titles and well-liked authors and illustrators. Focus on kid appeal and building book knowledge. Lean into students' observations and opinions, but support students as needed by modeling and teaching book-selection strategies.

As you get to know your students as people and readers, preview stacks will become more individualized and tailored to the needs, interests, and abilities of each reader. You will feel more confident spontaneously pulling books from the classroom library for them, too. The two of us often pull preview stacks from the classroom library during reading conferences to address a student need or interest.

Matching Calley With Books

While conferring with Levi, I noticed that Calley seemed to be struggling to engage with her book. She had recently told me that she really wanted to read a chapter book. Most of the books she had read during the first four months of the school year had been graphic novels. She decided to read *Hatchet* because she loved it when her fourth-grade teacher read it aloud to the class. I wasn't sure whether she was struggling to read it, or whether she was just having a tough reading day. I sat down next to her and asked her how reading was going for her. She told me that it was fine. I didn't respond. I just nodded and gave her some space to think and say more. After what seemed like a very long 20 or so seconds, she said, "Well, it's not really going fine. I'm bored and having a hard time paying attention to *Hatchet*."

I nodded again and smiled. "That's okay, Calley. This happens to all readers. Maybe I can help you find some books. Tell me a little bit about what you love about graphic novels and what you are looking for in a chapter book."

Calley felt that *Hatchet* had too many words on a page, and the small print was overwhelming her. She said that she would love a book where the characters played sports and that some pictures would be nice. I told her I would be back in a few minutes with a stack of books for her to preview.

I headed to the classroom library section that included series bins of illustrated novels. I grabbed the first book in the Stick Dog and Stick Cat series (by Tom Watson). These hybrid books are a nice mix of text and images with lots of white space on each page that I thought Calley might appreciate. I also grabbed a copy of Andy Griffiths and Terry Denton's *The 13-Story Treehouse*, Janet and Jake Tashjian's *My Life As a Book* and a few other illustrated novels. I didn't find any sports-centered books that included illustrations, but I knew that Kwame

Alexander's novels in verse—*Booked*, *Rebound*, and *The Crossover*—might appeal to her because many kids who played sports liked them. In the realistic fiction section of our classroom library, I grabbed Hena Khan's *Power Forward*, *On Point*, and *Bounce Back*. This series of books about an elementary kid chasing his hoop dreams just might be what Calley was looking for in a chapter book.

I brought the stack of books to the carpet where Calley was reading and briefly told her about the books. She seemed interested in a bunch of them and ultimately chose *Power Forward*. I told her she made a great choice! I invited her to place the book stack on top of a bookshelf in our classroom, so that she could go back to it later and add any more books to her to-read list that looked interesting to her.

Creating a preview stack for a student is a beneficial move any time you believe that a student struggles with successfully choosing books or feels overwhelmed by too many book choices. However, focus on students' independence and their development of self-selection strategies. You are not their personal book shopper! A preview stack is meant to lead them to series, authors, and books they might not realize meet their interests and needs, but you want students to take it from there.

Book Talks

In a survey of almost one thousand adult readers, most of them reported that their most reliable source of book recommendations was people they knew (Miller & Kelley, 2013). Book talks—short "commercials" for a book—provide entry points for students to discuss books. In a classroom community where all readers are welcome to share their opinions about books, book talks can connect readers. When the adults at school regularly exchange book talks with kids, we educators communicate some powerful messages: adults are reading, we care about which books you might like, and we are interested in your suggestions, too! Even when students are not interested in a particular book talk, we are modeling how to talk about books, they are learning more about books in general, and the readerly language used to describe and explain their reading, such as literary elements or the parts of a book.

Each day, set aside a few minutes at the beginning of your literacy block (or another transition time) for a book talk. Students will enjoy learning about "new-to-me" books, and you can select your book talks to advance your reading goals with students. Which genres or titles do your students avoid reading or overlook in the classroom library? Book-talk titles from less popular genres. Do your students gravitate toward newer books and series and skip older books they might enjoy? Book-talk some older titles you think kids might enjoy. Can you connect any books to other titles you have shared with the class? Same author, genre, or topic?

Getting the Most Out of Book Talks

You do not need to write a script or practice performing your book talk in a mirror, unless these strategies help your memory or boost your confidence. Remember that you are modeling how to talk about books with other readers, not to present a book report or perform a monologue. Your enthusiasm and heartfelt opinions are all you need. Jot down a few key points on a sticky note to keep the details straight.

Teachers never have enough time, and rituals such as book-talking often fall by the wayside when they're pressed for time. So, keep your book talks short and lively. Your goal is to entice kids to read the book. You are just giving them enough information to make an informed choice for themselves.

You do not have to finish a book before you book-talk it, but it helps. You will have a better grasp on who might enjoy a book if you read all of it. However, you do not need to read every book you invite kids to read. Choose a few poems, one short story, a few pages, or visuals. You are modeling for students how to preview and sample books, as well as encouraging them to read more.

Although kids appreciate it when we enthuse about a book we loved, our book talks must be selected with students' needs in mind, not just our reading experiences. Use book talks as an opportunity to expand students' reading horizons beyond the books they know. What topics interest them? How can you connect book-talk titles to books they already recognize? After finishing a read-aloud, share a few more books by the same author or illustrator.

Seek out book-talking models online. Major publishers create seasonal previews, book trailers, and interviews when releasing new books. Check out a few publishers' YouTube channels or Instagram accounts. Colby regularly book-talks popular books in his classroom or recent reads on his YouTube channel.

Decide how you will pass the books to students BEFORE book-talking. You never know which book will catch students' attention, and we have both been unprepared by an enthusiastic response to our book talks. What do you do when ten kids want to read a book now? In Donalyn's classes, students wrote their names on slips of paper, and she drew the next reader's name from a bag. You can use a randomizer app, too. Many teachers keep a reserve list for popular books on a clipboard in the classroom library.

The best people to recommend books to kids? Other kids! Turn over book-talking to your students as much as possible. Resist the urge to turn book talks into book report assignments, and encourage kids to share their heartfelt opinions about what they enjoy reading. Set aside 15-20 minutes once a week for book talks, or a shorter time each day. Colby's students often share book talks during their morning meeting time. Record short, spontaneous "one take" book talks with students using an iPad or other device and save these recordings for future classes or library patrons. After one school year, you will have hundreds of recommendations from kids. Book-talking not only increases students' knowledge of books—it forges reader-to-reader connections between kids.

First Chapter Fridays: Combining a Read-Aloud and a Book Talk!

Although we cannot track down the origin, First Chapter Fridays began as an activity for high school teachers who wanted to share new books with students but rarely had time for read-alouds or book talks because class time was limited. The practice is easy to implement. Teachers select a text they would like to promote for

independent reading or share with students, read aloud the first chapter and discuss it, and then offer up the book to someone who wants to read it. You can see how this practice combines the benefits of reading aloud and a book talk in a short amount of time.

Colby uses First Chapter Fridays (or Tuesdays, Wednesdays, and Thursdays) as an alternative to book talks and to mix up the routine. It's a quick and fun way to introduce a book, author, or series. After listening to the beginning of Jason Reynolds's *Ghost* for First Chapter Friday, Landon took it and became lost in the story.

During every free minute he had, Landon would pull out *Ghost* to see what happened next with main character Castle Crenshaw. Within a handful of days he had finished the book, then began reading *Patina*, the second book in the Track series. The same day that Landon started reading

Patina, Colby noticed that both Wyatt and Jett were reading *Ghost*. That small sample of *Ghost* sparked an interest in the series for several kids.

You never know when a book talk, a First Chapter Friday, or a preview stack is going to lead to a book making its way around a classroom.

From Book Talks to Displays and Lists

As the school year continues, you can observe how books and the reading experiences around them bring kids together. Books often connect kids who would not interact much otherwise. The two of us have seen students become more accepting of each other's differences in general when they become more accepting of each other as readers. Every person in the community belongs and contributes to the group. Kids who discover reading interests in common (or develop them during the school year) often forge relationships that extend beyond books. In a classroom community that values reading and readers' opinions about books, a lot of book discussions will take place without you.

Let Students Take the Lead

Conversations about books, as well as the continuous exchange of book recommendations and responses between students, are most potent when students take the lead. It is not possible for one teacher to drive the reading lives of an entire classroom of young readers, and we don't need to take on this controlling role. When students build confidence in their book knowledge and feel safe in the reading community, it is better for them to forge reader-to-reader relationships with their peers than depend on you for all their book discussions and choices.

When we promote books to our students, we don't just give them suggestions for books to read—we model how to talk about books so they can do it, too.

Book talks and other structured opportunities for students to share their book recommendations with a larger group can increase students' knowledge of the books available for them to read and allow them to celebrate the books they have enjoyed and forge deeper connections with peers who read. When kids talk about books, their reading interest and motivation increases (Cherry-Paul & Johansen, 2019). In classrooms where kids drive most of the book recommendations, your students will grow more independence for their reading lives and become more aware of their preferences.

Once students feel confident with your book-talk routines, offer additional ways for students to share their book recommendations. After reviewing their reading lists for the year, Donalyn's students jotted down book recommendations for her future sixth graders and posted them on the classroom library walls (Miller & Kelley, 2013). Colby's students create personal lists, which he collects in a class book.

Collect students' book talks throughout the year in a Google Sheet and share the list with families for summer reading suggestions. Instead of creating book lists and displays, which value your opinions about books over students' reading experiences, create a recommendation station in your classroom and invite students to take turns displaying a few of their favorite reads. Use Padlet to quickly collect and share book titles. As students move toward more independence for their reading lives, evaluate your book recommendation activities to ensure that all students feel encouraged to give their personal reactions to what they read.

Epicenter Readers and Student Expertise

In a classroom community, there are some students who are more knowledgeable about books and reading than others. Students may have been influenced by what the adults in their lives read or by the texts their teachers and librarian have shared, or they may have discovered many books on their own through the public library or school. Generally, kids who enjoy reading have regular access to books and some encouragement from adults. With a classroom library available, these engaged readers will expand their reading horizons by browsing the collection and collecting book recommendations. When books and reading become a significant part of the classroom culture, kids who enjoy reading a lot can positively influence the reading habits of their peers. They are "epicenter" readers.

Just like the epicenter of an earthquake or a cultural movement, readers' passion and book knowledge radiate from their epicenters and affect other readers around them (Miller & Kelley, 2013). Get to know your students and watch them in the classroom library. Which kids seem comfortable using the collection and are knowledgeable about books or authors? Do you have students who offer book suggestions or discuss books outside independent reading time or class conversations?

The two of us have often identified the epicenter readers in our rooms because of their interactions with us and other students the first few weeks of school. This past year, Colby noticed early on that Landon seemed to have a firm grasp on what he liked. He loved survival books and had read many Gary Paulsen books. His family purchased books written by his favorite survival TV star, Bear Grylls. Evaluating students' book knowledge and their book selection and discussion skills can reveal the epicenter readers in your midst.

Who brings their books from home or the library to show you? Who seeks you out for book conversations? Who recommends books to *you*? Epicenter readers grow in confidence when their reading communities value their expertise. But don't assume that epicenter readers don't need independent reading support just because they are enthusiastic. They may need additional support to launch conversations with other kids, or their reading tastes may be narrow—fascinated with fantasy but never reads nonfiction, for example. During reading conferences, consider how tapping into their enthusiasm for books can broaden their social and reading experiences.

In this chapter, we shared ideas for introducing the classroom library to students and welcoming them into an exciting and nurturing year of reading. As you continue to finesse routines such as book-talking and daily independent reading time, students will become more self-directed in their use of the classroom library. When they feel capable of finding books consistently, kids will navigate the library more often without you. In the final chapter, we will explore ways of encouraging students' burgeoning independence by tapping into their interactions with books and each other.

TIME TO REFLECT

- **What rituals and routines do you rely on to provide a variety of literacy experiences for students and support a classroom culture of reading?** What would you change about those rituals and routines? After reading this chapter, what are you interested in trying out or tweaking?

- **Select five students who would benefit from more support with book selection.** Create preview stacks of three to five books for each one of them. Use resources such as book lists and your school librarian to choose books for each stack. Confer with students and walk them through their preview stacks. What do you notice about students' previewing and evaluating strategies? Could each student find a book to read?

- **Consider your book-talking routines.** How can you leverage them to increase students' reading interest for books they avoid or unfamiliar books? What sections of the library need more book love? Select a book or two from genres students avoid or areas of the library they don't frequent. Did any students show interest? What did they think of the book or section after giving it a try? What types of readers do they think would appreciate the book? Why?

Responding to Students' Needs and Interests

With a foundation of classroom routines and rituals underway, such as book-talking and daily reading time, your students will grow more confident and capable of directing their own reading lives. No matter how supportive your classroom reading community might be, your students' time with you is temporary. They must become more independent *now*. As the National Council of Teachers of English (NCTE) asserts, "the purpose of independent reading is to build habitual readers with conscious reading identities" (2019). How are your students developing personal reading habits and behaviors, such as finding time to read and self-selecting books? How are students becoming more aware of themselves as readers—their preferences, goals, and gaps? Are they able to manage their own reading lives with some success and self-agency?

Observing students as they navigate the school and classroom libraries, conferring with them about their personal reading goals and challenges, giving them opportunities to reflect on their reading experiences and identities, and fostering reader-to-reader relationships between students moves them toward more independence as readers.

The classroom library is a ready resource for responding to students during a conference by allowing you to build preview stacks, find specific books, and browse sections of interest with a student. Colby's reading conference with Danny shows how students will challenge themselves as readers when given encouragement and support for their interests and choices.

Trying Out New Formats and New Authors

During a reading conference, Danny told me that he wanted to try reading a novel in verse. I asked him to tell me more, and he told me that he noticed a bunch of kids in the class were reading them. He wanted to see if he liked them, too. He mentioned that he had tried reading Sharon Creech's *Love That Dog* back in fourth grade, but he didn't really understand what was going on.

I grabbed *Love That Dog* from our classroom library to look at with Danny. I read the first few poems so that he could get a feel for what to do with the line breaks. Then I directed Danny to the back of the book to find the classic poems that Jack, the main character, was reading in class. Throughout *Love That Dog*, Jack responds to those poems for assignments and uses them as models for his own poems. If readers are unfamiliar with the poems or cannot locate them, a lot of the book can be confusing. Directing them to the poems helps.

Danny took the book and started reading the next poem. I looked up from the book to scan the classroom, and I noticed that Sophia was reading Sharon Creech's *The Boy on the Porch*. I hadn't thought about that book in years. I remembered really liking the book, but for some reason I had never purchased it for our classroom library.

Danny read a couple poems to me, then asked if he could continue on his own. I smiled as he headed back to his seat. He just needed a little support for figuring out how to read *Love That Dog,* and then he was ready to go.

Next, I had to ask Sophia about *The Boy on the Porch*. She told me that at the beginning of the year, she read both *Love That Dog* and *Hate That Cat*. From there she read another of the author's books, *Saving Winslow*. Looks like I had a Sharon Creech fan in the classroom! Sophia said that when we  visited the school library last week, she had found *The Boy on the Porch* while searching the shelves for more Sharon Creech books.

Before I moved on to my next conference, I thought about Danny bravely trying out a new format and author. Who knows where that will take him? A couple of months ago, Sophia took a chance and discovered a new favorite author. Offering choice and ready access to books encourages kids to expand their reading selections. Our classroom reading community supports that growth. Each book talk, recommendation, or nudge to try something new could lead readers to that one book, series, or author that deepens their love for reading.

As Colby confers with students, he can see that Danny, Sophia, and others are seeking out books in the school and classroom libraries, challenging themselves to try new things, and building preferences of their own. As their confidence grows, students will take more ownership for their reading choices, but they may need support for identifying manageable reading goals or gaps in their reading diets. Let's take a look at some conference points and activities that dig into students' reading habits, interests, and needs.

Reading Gaps and Goals

Even if you confer regularly with students about their independent reading, stop, take a breath, celebrate their reading accomplishments, and set goals for what comes next. When you ask students about their reading experiences and encourage their reading tastes and behaviors, you communicate respect. By providing opportunities for reflection, such as administering surveys, you allow students to express their opinions about books and reading and gain information about how best to move them forward. Be sure to inquire about their favorite authors, books, genres, and so on, as well as about their reading goals for themselves.

The two of us often survey students at the midway point in the school year—at the semester break or early in the calendar year. That's a good time for students to reflect on how much they have grown as readers and what they would like to try next. This is a nice activity for easing back into reading after a winter holiday break or long January weekend. Colby includes some of the same questions in his midyear survey that he includes in his check-in survey earlier in the year because he is interested in how students' responses to questions might have changed. By asking questions a second time, Colby hopes that kids will see how much they have evolved as readers.

COLBY'S CLASSROOM

Midyear Reading Reflection

Coming off a two-week winter break, my kids came into the room with arms filled with the stacks of books they had taken home to read. I was excited to see them, hear about how they spent their time away from school, and, of course, chat with them about their reading during our time apart.

As the room filled with kids, the energy was electric. Kids descended on the classroom library, returning books to bins and selecting books for independent reading. Other kids dropped school library books into the class return tub. I overheard kids talking about going sledding, their favorite holiday presents, and the books they read. Landon chatted with Kent about Kwame Alexander's *The Crossover* and three graphic novels about sports that he found in our school library. Zander shared how proud of himself he was for reading all of the books in Thomas Flintham's Press Start series.

I chatted with Jessie, who told me that she didn't read as much as she would have liked. She read almost every day, but she was bummed that her busy schedule didn't allow her to read for long. She tried to steal reading time whenever she could and found some interesting ways to do it. The image of her reading aloud Katherine Applegate's *The One and Only Bob* to the cow she's raising for 4-H is an image that I will never forget! I told her I was proud of her for always finding a little bit of time to read.

Looking Back and Looking Forward

Later in the day, I shared with my fifth graders how my reading went over the break. I book-talked John David Anderson's *Riley's Ghost* and Erin Entrada Kelly's *Those Kids From Fawn Creek*, two books I had read and enjoyed. I told them that my reading life over the break had its peaks and valleys. Some days I read for five minutes, and other days I read for a few hours. I don't ever want my fifth graders to believe that my reading life is perfect and magical every day. From there, I handed out a reading reflections sheet. The sheet was filled with questions that would guide kids to reflect on their winter break reading, look back at their reading during the school year so far, and begin to set reading goals going forward.

A couple of the questions that I asked were repeats of questions I asked in a prior survey this year: "What are some of your favorite books that you have read so far this year?" "What are some books you are planning to read in the future?" I also asked them again to share something they have learned about themselves as readers. Their answers were fascinating:

- Now I know that I am not the best reader ever, but at least I read here. This is the one place I can read without an annoyance.
- I learned that reading is actually better than what it seems like.
- I like fantasy—to be specific I like scary books. I also like graphic novels.
- I've learned that I have read more this year than last year.
- I never liked to read, but when I came to fifth grade I started to like reading. I never thought I would be a good reader.
- I like reading a lot more than I used to. I like fantasy and poetry and graphic novels.
- I'm starting to read different books rather than just graphic novels.
- I learned that there are many books for me to read.

These responses showed me that they are really starting to understand themselves as readers, and I felt like I have some places to go the next time I sit down with each kid during a reading conference.

A new prompt on the midyear survey that I did not give them previously was, "List three authors you like." When I asked them to do that the first week of school, many students couldn't answer. I got a lot of vague responses such as, "The author that writes the Dog Man books and the one that writes Diary of a Wimpy Kid." I had hoped they might read multiple books by an author they discovered—just like readers do outside of school. Finding an author they can connect with goes a long way toward keeping some kids reading. I was pretty pumped to see authors such as Abby Cooper, Jason Reynolds, Kwame Alexander, Sharon Draper, and Hena Khan on kids' surveys. Some kids still struggled to answer that question, and I made a note to chat with them about their tastes in authors during our next reading conference.

Because we were halfway through the year, I also wanted to know more about which genres my students were reading and which they were avoiding. Based on survey data, only 32 percent of my readers had read a biography, 92 percent of them had read a realistic fiction book, and 100 percent of the kids had read at least one graphic novel. No surprises there. Again, this data was very helpful for me to see a whole-class picture of the books we were reading, and it gave me lots of ideas of where I could go with individual reading conferences.

I knew that most of my kids were relying pretty heavily on our classroom and school libraries to find the books that they read. If you were surrounded by books and readers, you'd probably read the books in front of you, too. Especially when your peers were book-talking those books to you daily!

Planning for Reading Outside of School

To help my students find more books to read when they could not rely on our classroom library anymore, I also asked kids to tell me where they'd been getting their reading material in the last few months. I wasn't surprised to learn that 96 percent of my students had read books from our classroom library and 72 percent had read books from our school library. I was concerned that only 24 percent had read books that they got from home and only 4 percent had checked out a book from the public library. We still had time in the year to address this gap, but I wanted to keep my eye on students' access points as we continued to move kids toward more independence from the classroom library and me.

In the final question on the reflection sheet, I asked my kids to share how reading was going for them outside of school. I knew that many of them were struggling with this habit. I wanted them to put into words what was giving them trouble, so that we could problem-solve during our next reading conferences. Since many of kids admitted reading at home was a challenge, I dedicated some whole-class time to talk about what was working, what wasn't working, and what readers could do to find more time to read at home. I think that many of my readers who were not reading consistently outside of school felt a little better when they realized they weren't alone.

Using Survey Responses to Guide Reading Conferences

Over the next seven school days, I met with every kid in a reading conference. During the conferences, we talked about their reflection responses and dug into their goals as readers. Wyatt read Rodman Philbrick's *Wild River* and Ibi Zoboi's *My Life as an Ice Cream Sandwich* over winter break. He felt proud when he looked back at all the books he had read during the school year, and he told me that his goal was to read more about topics that interested him. This moment, he was interested in outer space. We talked about where he might find books about outer space in our classroom and school libraries. Kent finished Katherine Applegate's *The One and Only Ivan* and Jason Reynolds's *Sunny*. He was surprised that he ran out of books to read and decided that he would make sure he took home more books when spring break rolled around. Kent asked whether we had any books about soccer or manatees in the classroom library. We looked and struck out. From there, I pulled up the website for our local public library and walked Kent through how to put books on hold. We reserved two books about manatees and Bonnie Bader's *What Is the World Cup?* I would pick them up later. During both conferences, I pulled out my running list of "books we need" and added a note about outer space, manatees, and soccer books.

During Danny's conference, he had shared how much harder it was for him to read at home than in class. He said it was easy to read when everyone around you was reading, but that at home there were a lot more distractions. I told him that I often felt the same way. We brainstormed ways he could limit distractions so that he could get into the same reading groove at home.

Daltin talked about how he read in his dad's semi truck when they went on a long-haul trip together. I praised him for remembering to take books with him on the road. He mentioned that he had been thinking a lot about working on cars and trucks, and that he'd like it if we had some books about mechanics in our school or classroom library. I added it to the list and made a mental note to talk with our librarian.

As I worked my way through conferences, I noticed some trends:

- Kids were thinking about genres they hadn't read much this year. Many of my students had not yet read much poetry or nonfiction. We were studying nonfiction during our daily mini-lessons, and kids were becoming more interested in reading it.

- Kids were reading more outside of school. Not all of my students read a lot during break, but most of them read at least half the days. Reading was becoming something they did because they found personal value in it, not something they did just for school.

- They were starting to see the limitations of our classroom library. It is impossible for a classroom library to have every book for every reader, and my kids were starting to look elsewhere to locate the books they wanted to read. This made me happy. We only have about five months left together, and the more independently they can find books, the more likely they will continue to do so in the summer.

- Our reading community supports each other. Time and again, kids mentioned that the reason they read a specific book over vacation was because a classmate had read it and recommended it. It was encouraging to see them transition from depending on me to find great books for them to relying on each other for recommendations.

When Donalyn and I were discussing the recent death of author and illustrator Steve Jenkins, Donalyn mentioned a video she used to show her students. In it, Jenkins creates illustrations for one of his books and talks with kids about his process. After finding myself captivated by the video, I stopped by the school library to check out several Steve Jenkins books. My students loved the video and couldn't get enough of his books. I added Steve Jenkins's name to our "Books We Need" List. I thought it would be cool to create an author tub for him in our classroom library because kids had shown such an interest.

When I went over to the nonfiction section of our classroom library, I realized that we didn't have many author tubs there. Yikes! I made a note to create two to four more tubs for nonfiction authors in our classroom library. I was beginning to see why so few of my readers were reading nonfiction books. While the library has a large section of nonfiction books, I wasn't featuring nonfiction authors and titles as well as I was featuring fiction authors and titles.

Kids Shape the Classroom Library

The next step in my midyear check-in with readers and our classroom library was to do some weeding. Donalyn and I had done a lot of that work in the summer, but I wanted to take a quick walkthrough and decide whether any books could be pulled to make room for some of the

new titles we had added in the first semester. The first thing I noticed was that the realistic fiction tubs for authors whose last names begin with the letter *R* were bursting at the seams. I added another tub, and moved some books over to it, but quickly realized that most of the new tub was filled with books by Jason Reynolds. Donalyn and I chatted about it, and I decided to move Jason's books to their own tub and moved him to the author section of our classroom library. Reynolds's Track series was hugely popular, and I was hoping that putting them together with his other books would lead Track readers to books such as *Look Both Ways* and *Stuntboy, in the Meantime*.

Moving around the library, I pulled books that I hadn't seen kids reading this year or last year. I placed these books in two piles: books to weed and books to book-talk. Not all the books kids weren't reading were books they wouldn't like—some were books kids just didn't know about yet. A quick book talk might get some of those books into the hands of happy readers. This weeding round didn't take three days, as it did in the summer. I was able to make my way through the library in a little over an hour. I found a few dozen books to book-talk over the next couple of weeks and about a hundred books to retire from the classroom library. My hope was that removing some of the books kids weren't reading from the library might help them find books they do want to read.

Reading habits and preferences surveys, such as the ones Colby administers to his kids, gives a snapshot of students' reading interests, behaviors, and plans at this moment in time. You can also identify any issues that may still be preventing students from accessing books or self-selecting books they can read and enjoy. Examining a student's individual responses to your survey can inform your next conversation or reading conference, but wait until you talk with them before drawing too many conclusions from their answers to your questions. What do you notice about their responses, and how do they mesh (or not) with your understanding of this student as a reader? What questions do you have for them?

Surveys to Identify Trends

Ultimately, surveys give students time and space to reflect on their reading identities and personal goals for reading and provide you with information to support them as readers. They can also give you a snapshot of reading interests and trends across your entire class. What do you notice? What formats, authors, and genres seem popular with groups of students this year? What surprises you? What confirms your understandings? How can what you learn influence your lesson plans, book purchases, and read-alouds? Do your students' responses reflect a need for more book-talking in certain areas? More book passes?

Surveys give students time and space to reflect on their reading identities and personal goals for reading and provide you with information to support them as readers.

Share with students how you will use survey responses to make adjustments and additions to the classroom library. This is important because often, students tell us that surveys make them nervous because they do not know how the information will be used. Share survey information with parents and caregivers as appropriate, too, and solicit their feedback. What do they notice about their child's reading habits and attitudes now? What has changed since the school year began?

Reading Plans to Keep the Momentum Going

Like many of you, the two of us are always looking for our next book to read. When we confer with young readers, though, they sometimes have only vague ideas about their next book. Independent, self-directed readers see themselves as readers now and visualize themselves reading in the future. For them, planning for reading means planning to be a reader (Miller & Kelley, 2013). Whether or not readers follow through on their reading plans, they benefit from considering what to read and looking forward to reading. While reading plans differ from reader to reader, we've noticed similarities or common themes among them.

Planning to Invest More Time in Reading

Adults and kids alike say they do not have a daily reading habit and cannot find consistent time to read. Without habitual reading, it is difficult for students to read in volume. As Colby found, many of his students expressed a desire to read more outside school. When students do not show adequate developmental progress or express negative attitudes about reading in class, confer with them about their reading habits at home. What obstacles may prevent them from reading as much as they would like? Work with families to provide stable access to books and any assistive technology needed to read. Kids cannot read much when they do not have anything to read—it doesn't matter how much reading time they can find.

When making a commitment to read more, adults will increase access for themselves by acquiring library cards, downloading ebooks or audiobooks, or subscribing to newspapers and magazines, blogs, or newsletters. You can support students' plans to read more by ensuring their access to texts.

Planning to Finish a Book You've Started

Sometimes, readers start a book and do not finish it. Donalyn refers to this as "putting a book on pause." You are not reading it, but you are not ready to abandon it either. Many lifelong readers abandon books when they do not meet their mercurial needs. The book was not a good fit for whatever reason. With students, we find it helpful to consider where in the book students abandoned it. If the reader bailed on the book in the first few chapters, we would work with them on book-selection strategies and reflect with them about why their choice didn't work this time. It happens. When a student stops reading a book after the halfway mark, we wonder whether they lack the endurance necessary to stick with a longer text, need comprehension strategies and support, or do not have enough background knowledge about the text's topics or language use.

> When making a commitment to read more, adults will increase access for themselves.... You can support students' plans to read more by ensuring their access to texts.

Planning to Read Specific Books, Series, Authors, and Illustrators

Just like Sophia and her newfound love for Sharon Creech, readers discover authors, illustrators, and series that resonate with them. It is great when kids can develop some knowledge of authors and illustrators who write books for their age, especially when those authors write across age groups. Kids can grow up with authors such as Renée Watson and Jacqueline Woodson, who they "meet" in elementary school and keep reading for many years after. Same with series. Kids like to read series because they provide the comfort of familiar characters, plots, or text structures. Kids tell us that reading a series means they don't have to think about what they are going to read next, which they find stressful. Talking with many adult readers, they often identify a series they read as a child or teen as a special reading memory or a turning point in their reading lives where they fell in love with books.

Keeping a to-read list helps students keep track of any books they hear or read about that they are interested in reading. In a classroom or school where the book buzz is constant, it can be hard to keep up with all of the recommendations. Circling back to their to-read lists can remind kids of specific books they showed interest in reading.

Planning to Read for Learning or Personal Growth

Reading often sparks further reading or inquiry (Miller & Lesesne, 2022). Students may discover a passionate interest after reading a book and want to pursue more books on the subject, or they may learn about an historical period and want to read from different perspectives, and so on. Other readers may want to learn a skill, such as baking cupcakes or knitting scarves. Kids have many different options for learning, but with ready access to books every day, they learn that books are places they can go to learn and expand their minds.

Connecting Readers With Books

One of the greatest benefits of the classroom library is the proximity to books it provides to teachers and students throughout the school day. When you allow students to freely browse books and discuss them with their peers, you offer them low-risk opportunities to practice book selection and discussion skills. Having a ready collection of books that support instruction and students' independent

reading choices helps you respond to in-the-moment needs for books to use in a lesson or hand to a reader.

As third-grade teacher Lynsey Burkins describes, fingertip access to books in the classroom library provides her with lots of opportunities to connect her students with books by matching their interests and needs in real time.

Using the Classroom Library as Your Co-Teacher

Lynsey Burkins

Donalyn: Lynsey, you've talked about how your classroom library is like a co-teacher because you're dipping in and out of it all day long—tying it to your instruction in ways that are perhaps unplanned and spontaneous. Can you talk a bit about that cycle of instruction, read-aloud, and independent reading and how the classroom library supports it?

Lynsey: A lot of my trips in and out of the library are spontaneous. Right now, I have a student teacher, and I'm trying to make explicit what she can't see. It's hard! But I tell her that I know this classroom library. I've curated it, so I know a lot of these books. When I'm having conversations with kids, I already know that one of my goals is to connect them with some piece of literature.

When we're in writing workshop, when I notice a kid trying a new craft move, I always try to link them with an author who I've seen try the same moves. If I don't know of one, I will ask the kid, "Have you read anything lately that makes you think of this? How does the author do it?" It's that spontaneous linking that just happens.

Throughout the day, the classroom library is our guide. The literature is the piece where we come together and form that community of thinking and analyzing what the author is trying to teach us about ourselves and the world.

Donalyn: So is this why teachers need a classroom library? Because one book just can't do it?

Lynsey: It can't do it. Also, kids need books for independent reading.

Donalyn: Teachers and kids can't go to the library as much as we would need to. One book won't do it. From what you just described, let's not even count kids' independent reading books. You probably read nine texts a day with your kids in various ways.

Colby: Some of the books that you're going to talk about tomorrow, you probably already know, or you will know, when the bell rings in the morning. And half of the books or more that you will talk about tomorrow—that will be a part of your day with kids—you will have no idea until those moments arise.

Lynsey: Exactly. That's it. That's what it is.

Ease with using the classroom library often fosters students' confidence and curiosity to seek books elsewhere. For students, access to the classroom library often leads to more school and public library use. The two of us have seen this with our own students. Colby noticed that kids begin to seek out book recommendations from their peers and other sources such as the librarian. The classroom library could never meet every reader's needs, and it is not meant to do so. In many ways, the classroom library has more in common with a home library—a small collection that serves a limited number of readers. The classroom library is a space where students can practice their book selection skills, chat with peers about books and reading, and learn how to preview and evaluate books. Using a classroom library all the time increases students' comfort with larger collections, such as the school library and public library. Ideally, our students would all have library cards and access to the public library in their communities.

As the year comes to an end, Colby looks for opportunities for students to reflect on their reading lives, celebrate their reading experiences for the school year, and plan for future reading. Inviting students to share a timeline of their reading lives guides them to explore the positive and negative experiences that have shaped them as readers. Throughout this project, students show support for each other's histories and opinions. This type of activity works best when students have built reader-to-reader relationships together.

My Reading Life Project

Classroom libraries can play a large positive role in a child's reading life. One of the favorite reading reflection activities in my class is the Reading Life Project. I invite students to share as much as they want about their reading lives so far. They can share the books they have enjoyed, the read-alouds they remember, and the negative experiences they've had with reading, too. They can write about them and create a comic, poster, video, or something in another format. After sharing my reading life with them as a model, they get to work. My students' reading-life projects have provided me with so much information about the conditions and actions that bring kids to reading, and the things that push them away from books.

Nolan was one of the happiest kids that I have taught. His reading life project showed images of him happily reading each year of his life. He read with his parents, his teachers, by himself, and with his classmates. In each picture, Nolan held a book and wore a giant smile on his face. For Nolan, being a part of a reading community meant the world to him. As long as he was in the presence of other readers, reading was something that brought him joy.

One student shared how her third-grade teacher read aloud Katherine Applegate's *The One and Only Ivan* and made her fall in love with books that were filled with drama. She fell into a bit of a reading rut after that read-aloud, but once she got to my classroom, she rediscovered her interest. A teacher who supported her reading choices and led her to books like *The One and Only Ivan* brought her back to reading. It is not enough to just have books in your room. I know the books in my classroom, and I have read hundreds, if not thousands, of them. I am aware of many books that we do not have in the room. This knowledge helps me recommend books to my readers—whether they need to find their way back to books, they want to try something new, or they are developing an interest in reading for the first time.

Want to know one of the most heartbreaking trends I see among my former students? How many of them go from reading up a storm one year to hardly reading at all the next. I run into my former students often, and I ask them what happened if they tell me they are not reading. The most common reason they experienced a difficult reading year was because they did not have access to books that they wanted to read in their language arts classrooms.

Madilynn drew a picture of a book with a big X through it on her reading-life project. She titled that year of her reading life: NO BOOKS. Dan wrote about how he fell in love with the graphic novel series Amulet during one school year, but said that during the next school year, his classroom didn't have any good books. He went on to say that his mom took him to the library that year to get the graphic novels that he wanted to read. Not all kids have parents like Dan's who are able to take them to the library. The more that I hear these heartbreaking stories, the more I think about what would happen if kids were surrounded by books every year that they were in school. What if every classroom had a strong classroom library, and every school had a certified school librarian with a large book budget?

While having a robust classroom library filled with books kids want to read is important, the work doesn't stop there. For her project, Natalie wrote about how she had the highest reading level in her class, but she barely read and wasn't interested in any of the books in her classroom. Is this what we want?

While completing her reading-life project, Natalie realized that she had never thought of herself as someone who was encouraged to love reading, because she was shown that what mattered was her "reading level."

Is a high reading level satisfactory if a child has no interest in reading? I hope not. Natalie went on to say that being a part of our reading community has helped her read a ton of books and that she has discovered that she can love reading.

Alan is one of the most unforgettable readers that I have ever met. He came into my classroom as a new student in third grade. He was terrified when he saw all the books. Every reading experience in his life had been negative. He was retained in early elementary school and pulled out of class for extra reading instruction. To Alan, reading was nothing but heartache. In his reading-life project, Alan talked about how he started reading Mo Willems' Elephant & Piggie books in third grade and eventually fell in love with reading when we studied picture books during our Mock Caldecott unit. I taught Alan in both third and fifth grades. In fifth grade, he started a book club that met weekly in my classroom. The love of books that he had developed had spread to other readers in our classroom.

Each year when I have kids reflect on their reading lives, the themes remain the same. When they are surrounded by books they want to read and given time and encouragement to read them, they fall deeper in love with reading. Without this support, their love for reading is jeopardized.

While the classroom library offers students books to read, it provides much more. It communicates the message that kids' reading lives are valued—that their opinions about books and reading are important and their voices matter. A curated classroom library feeds your efforts to connect kids with books. Eventually, you can see the classroom community become an organic influence on almost every reader in the room. Kids may browse the classroom library less and seek out peer recommendations more often. They may pass books to each other or help each other find books in the school library or classroom without you. All of these signs show that students are taking more control of their reading lives and developing personal reasons for reading.

Connecting Readers With Each Other

Students benefit from reading relationships with their peers. Even one friend who enjoys the same books they do can keep them interested in reading. You can't direct the reading lives of your entire class, and there's no need to. But fostering reader-to-reader connections between and among students can support them during the school year and beyond.

How Does a Reading Community Benefit Readers?

School communities that celebrate reading, model joyful reading habits, and encourage young people's choices positively influence them to read more and find more enjoyment from reading. For students who are BIPOC, an inclusive reading community can be even more important because these students and their families are often marginalized or poorly represented in traditional language arts classes and literacy programs (Johnson & Parker, 2020). The influence of families cannot be pushed aside.

In a survey of 1,000 adult readers, the majority identified a family member as the most significant reading influence of their lives (Miller & Kelley, 2013). This means that a strong school community must prioritize families' literacy experiences and needs (Mapp, Carver, & Lander, 2017; Vu, 2021). Children benefit when the adults in their lives show positive attitudes about reading. How adults talk about books and reading can influence kids' perception of reading, too. As Stephen Krashen (2004), Gholdy Muhammad (2020), and other scholars remind us, kids read more when they see other people reading (and enjoying it). Working with many readers and observing trends in their attitudes and behaviors, the two of us can identify some of the consistent benefits of participating in reading communities:

Reading communities forge connections between readers. When kids receive positive messages from both peers and adults, they are likely to read more and show more engagement with reading. For kids who love reading, a few bookish friends can become a consistent source of book recommendations and conversations about books. Those who do not yet find reading enjoyable may be drawn in through social interactions with other readers in the class.

Reading communities increase time spent reading. Regular reading has a strong correlation to reading test scores and increases readers' vocabulary and background knowledge. When teachers dedicate daily time for reading, we communicate to students the importance of reading. Kids will spend more time reading when they have peers who model a daily reading habit (Mansor, et al, 2012). When reading is part of the class culture, everyone reads more.

Reading communities suggest a lot of books to read. Students' discussions and interactions around books provide an endless source for book recommendations. All readers are valued, and their opinions about books matter in this community! These conversations provide authentic opportunities for students to talk about books and reading. Kids learn about a lot of books they might read from kids their own age—who may enjoy reading, but possess different tastes and preferences. Kids are respected and their books are respected here. All books have something to offer readers.

Reading communities challenge readers to read outside of their comfort zones. When teachers guide students to consider their reading tastes and choices, and classroom discussions hinge on books and reading, kids become more ambitious about challenging themselves as readers. Kids will set goals to read a series and talk about it with their friends or pursue a topic of interest by reading all of the shark books in the school library. When kids set reading challenges for themselves and meet them, they feel more comfortable stretching themselves.

Reading communities inspire more intentional reading and sharing. Instead of randomly selecting books during library day and reading them in isolation, in a thriving reading community, readers select books with more intention—accessing their own preferences and their knowledge about books. Because their personal opinions about books are important, kids acknowledge the preferences of other readers and consider what they know about each other when making book recommendations.

Reading communities influence readers' appreciation and comprehension of what they read. As we have mentioned, many people are social readers who enjoy reading more when they can share conversations about books and exchange recommendations with each other. Beyond social readers, though, studies show that literate conversations with peers can improve students' understanding of their reading and increase reading motivation (Nystrand, 2006; Cherry-Paul & Johansen, 2019). Listening to other readers' perspectives and impressions of a book—say in a book club group or informal chat with a friend—can provide additional experiences and ideas to consider.

The classroom library becomes the literacy hot spot in the classroom when the reading community takes hold. Kids dip in and out of the library to look for books for themselves, but they are just as likely to grab a book to show a classmate. The class, made of many different people with different reading interests, provides a variety of readers to talk with and seek out book recommendations. Looking for a fantasy book? Talk to Catherine—she loves anything with maps and unicorns in it. Curious about football? Go ask Jacob about that book of stats he was reading last week. It is magical to watch kids become the book "experts" in the room as they build confidence in their own reading identities and respect for the reading identities of their classmates. When kids find a peer group that shares and enhances their book love, they rely on adults less for book recommendations and validation. Kids feel more empowered and self-directed when they learn in a community that uplifts and embraces them. The two of us constantly remind ourselves that the goal of all teaching is independence. What we teach our readers today can last them for a lifetime. Our reading community is short-lived, but the reading experiences we have shared can carry our readers forward.

Middle school English teacher Katherine Sokolowski leverages her classroom library to entice her middle schoolers to read by encouraging self-selection and stocking the collection with high interest books. Katherine understands how to influence her middle schoolers' reading choices, but she recognizes that the conversations and interactions around books between her students encourage them even more.

Working With Middle School Readers

Katherine Sokolowski

Colby: How is working with your readers now similar or different from when you were an elementary teacher?

Katherine: In fifth grade, I had a few kids who read some young adult books like *The Hunger Games*, for example, which is a little bit of a reach. In seventh grade, the kids are at the top age for middle grade books and the bottom age for young adult books. My middle schoolers are straddling that line.

In fifth grade, with my students who began reading young adult books, it was hard to get them to go back and read middle grade books. It was like a status thing. They were young adult readers now. My seventh graders are more comfortable reading a YA book one day and middle grade the next. I brought a bunch of stuffed animals from my elementary classroom. My seventh graders like to read with the stuffed animals tucked in their arms. So, the seventh graders still deal with emotional upheaval—just like elementary kids—but many are more confident in who they are as readers. They are fine reaching back for a book that they found comforting when they were younger.

Middle Schoolers Thrive in a Safe and Inclusive Reading Community

Katherine: Because they know themselves better as readers, they know whether a book is too much of a reach for them right now, too. They are better at opting out of a book. I tell them that I have books on the shelves they might not be comfortable reading, but the same books might be good for another reader. I remember a girl last year in my class who picked up a book that had some rough language in it. She looked up from it at one point and said, "This is not a book for me." I said, "OK, what do you need to do?"

She said, "I am just going to put it back and get a different one."
I feel that seventh graders are capable of choosing books for
themselves, and our classroom library reflects that.

Donalyn: You have created a classroom space where students may feel
more comfortable in their own skins. The conditions you have
created—where choices are valued—offer kids more room to
express their reading preferences. You create such a nurturing
environment. I have been in a lot of middle school classrooms,
and kids are not walking around with stuffed animals and in touch
with their feelings all the time!

Give yourself a little credit for the culture that you have created.
Of course, the kids benefit from the collection that you have
curated, too. You have a collection that includes such a wide
range of books. You are giving kids implicit permission to read as
widely as they want—not just of the genres and the formats that
you put in the classroom library, but also the age ranges. You're
saying to the kids, "It is all there, and whatever you want to read
is fine with me."

Katherine: I think talking about content and feeling safe is part of building
relationships, right? I think that it's important, first, to give them
the language to talk about books. I start the year talking with my
students about Bishop's mirrors, windows, and sliding glass doors
and why representation and reading widely are important. Those
conversations help bridge the idea that the content of some
books may not be something that matches with your interests,
but that we are not censoring books in our room. And we are not
shaming anybody for anything they read.

Donalyn: You need a classroom library with as wide a variety and range of
books as possible in order to truly meet the needs of the kids that
you have. In seventh grade, you probably have kids at all stages of
emotional development in your classes. You want books for all of
them, but it is not just about the books. You want all of your kids
to feel like they belong.

Colby: Why do you think that so often, when kids get to be middle schoolers, some kids don't read as much as they did when they were younger?

Hearing you talk about books that your seventh graders are reading and how kids are recommending books, and this culture of reading within your classroom and school—how do you make that happen? Why is this not happening for more middle schoolers?

Katherine: I think there are a couple things. Kids are busier. Finding time for kids to read is critical. They have to read in class, and I ask my students to read outside of class, too. I encourage them to read a certain number of minutes per week, but we discuss that they might read on the weekends and steal reading time whenever they can. Conferring with them, I am looking for progress from one Friday to the next. You have to build reading time into class because it helps create a culture in the class where it is cool to read.

I work hard sometimes to get certain kids to buy in, because status is a thing in middle school. I had a boy in class two years ago who was popular. He asked, since he knew I was writing romance novels, "Do boys read romance?" And I said, "Of course they do." He said, "I could probably learn something about romance." I told him that the most popular romance novel in class was Jenny Han's *To All the Boys I've Loved Before*. I suggested he try it. He came back a few days later and said, "Well, that was amazing!" He started book-talking it to all the boys he knew might be interested, telling them, "If you want a girlfriend some day, you should read this book." That was his takeaway—that some boys could learn from these books and use it to their advantage! His stepbrother is in my class this year. First thing, he said, "My brother says I need to check out some books by a woman named Jenny."

Connecting students with books is fun. I try to message kids through Google Classroom when I find a book that I think they might be interested in reading. Just try to hook the kids any way you can while they are in school, but also, don't penalize them or get mad because of their out-of-school obligations. We need to look at the whole child. For some kids, athletics keeps them coming to school. For others, it is band. I try to respect that and get to know each kid and their passionate interests, because that helps me recommend books to them.

If my students see gaps in our classroom library—books and topics they want, but cannot find—we investigate what books might meet their needs. We search online bookstores and our little bookstore in town. My students see the power of being able to search for and track down books that they want to read.

Katherine's efforts to help her students locate books on their own remind us all that the goal of independent reading is to launch readers who can successfully self-select books and direct their own reading lives (Miller & Kelly, 2013; NCTE, 2019). As Colby's school year with his students draws to a close, he develops culminating activities that allow kids time and space to reflect on their reading experiences during the year and plan for future reading.

Letting Readers Go

While many teachers design culminating activities and projects as the school year ends, the two of us focus on activities that invite students to reflect on their reading accomplishments, celebrate their growth, and share their enthusiasm for books with one another. Many schools and libraries host summer events and programs to encourage kids and families to read.

For summer reading to happen, kids need tangible reading plans and book access. Cheerful encouragement such as, "Make sure you read over the summer," followed by no commitment from kids does not cut it. Work with students to identify specific books they want to read and figure out how to get some of those books into their hands before the school year ends. Ask them to make book lists and collect the books on their lists that they want to read most. Share the lists with your students and their families for summer reading and keep them at the ready for your future students, who will appreciate suggestions from other kids their age. Colby's students create end-of-year book lists as both a reflection and sharing activity.

The End-of-Year List Project

From November to January is an exciting time in children's and young adult literature because of the landslide of book awards and "Best of…" lists coming out. From *The New York Times*/New York Public Library Best Illustrated Children's Books List, to the American Library Association's Annual Youth Media Awards, to state awards lists, to the Nerdy Book Club Nerdies, the end of the year is an awesome time to be a reader. I often find myself adding dozens of books to my to-read list. When my favorite books of the year appear on notable book lists, I feel a sense of pride in my heart.

The end of our school year comes in late spring or early summer. This is a great time to celebrate the books we've fallen in love with by giving out our own book awards and creating book lists. At the end of every school year, each class votes on a different book award to hand out. We always choose one favorite picture book of the year and one favorite chapter book read-aloud. Other awards the kids have chosen include favorite author/illustrator, favorite series, funniest book, and best graphic novel. Kids nominate their favorites to create the ballot, and then we vote. Once we've selected our winners, I lay out each winning book open to the end papers. In each book, I write something like, "Mr. Sharp's 2021–2022 Class's Favorite Read-Aloud." Then, each kid signs all this year's winners. These books return to the classroom library for future readers to enjoy. Jon Klassen's *I Want My Hat Back*, Dan Santat's *The Adventures of Beekle: The Unimaginary Friend*, and Deborah Freedman's *The Story of Fish & Snail* have all taken home the top prize for best picture book and remain class favorites.

I don't usually tell my new classes about these end-of-year awards. It's more fun to wait until a kid discovers one of the winning books on their own, sees all the kids' signatures inside, and asks me about it. Such a discovery usually happens within the first month of the school year.

Learning that a book won an award—from kids their own age—invites a lot of kids to line up and read the book.

When we vote for our class favorites, many of the books my students have nominated do not win. In this moment of disappointment and comparison, I introduce our end-of-the-year awards project to the class. In that way, each reader will have a chance to personally lift up some books they have enjoyed and encourage others to read them. Kids create a book list to share with other kids—both their classmates and my new students next year. Over the years, my students have enjoyed this project because their influence lingers long after they leave my class. They are still part of the class—still sharing book recommendations—through their lists. Kids are excited about featuring some of the books that didn't make the cut for our class book awards on their lists. Here is a general overview of how the project runs:

Day One

Kids spend time looking at published book lists as models for writing their own. Many of them are familiar with the book list collections from my previous classes because they have used them. These bound book lists live in the classroom library, and kids often enjoy reading them and adding books to their to-read lists. I also print out lists and share links from sources like The Nerdy Book Club blog, the Schu/Jonker Top 20 Picture Book list, the ALA's Youth Media Awards, and the Michigan Library Association's Book Award lists.

Day Two

We discuss and write down what we notice about these published lists and awards. I jot down notes on chart paper. From there, we brainstorm topics for possible book lists. Some topics kids have come up with:

- Favorite Graphic Novels
- Best Read-Alouds
- Books That Will Scare Your Pants Off
- Awesome Dog Books Where the Dog Doesn't Die
- Best Series

Day Three

Kids select a book list topic. Before they dive in with the first idea that pops into their heads, I ask them to reflect on their own reading experiences during the school year and look over their genre graph and reading list in their reading binders. What do they notice about their own reading this year? Is there a way to connect topically some of the books they've read?

Walking around the room, providing support as needed, I overhear kids' thoughts about their list topics:

- "Whoa. I read 16 realistic books this year. Maybe I could make a list of my favorites."
- "I read the entire Track series by Jason Reynolds and all of Abby Cooper's books."
- "I wonder if I could do a list of awesome authors every fifth grader should know."
- "I'm a graphic novel expert. I should probably do a top graphic novel series book list."

During my rounds, two kids will almost always come up to me and say, "We both really love scary books. Could we do a "Top 10 Scary Books" list?" I smile and encourage them to create an epic scary book list. I try to avoid suggesting that kids partner up for this project at the beginning because it would inevitably lead to kids partnering up with their friends, then struggling to find a list they could write together. When a partnership develops more organically, these pairings lead to stronger collaborations that create awesome book lists.

After kids have selected their book list topics, they spend the rest of the time choosing books for their lists.

Day Four

I set two goals for this day. First, kids should finalize their book choices for their lists. Many of them are close to finishing their lists after our project session on Day Three. Once they have settled on their lists (for the most part), we gather as a group and share my personal "Best Books..." list topic and the books I have chosen for it. Next, I model writing an introduction that I hope will entice a reader to dig into my list.

The kids and I discuss different aspects of writing an introduction for their book lists, and they go off to write their own. I remind them to review some of the book lists we have studied at the beginning of the project.

After some writing time, we come back together, and a few volunteers share their book list introductions.

Days Five and Six

We kick off these workdays with a review of what readers appreciate about book talks. What information is helpful to persuade other readers? I write a model for one of the books on my book list. I always choose at least one book for my list that we have read together as a class, and we write a short review for it together. After this modeling and shared practice, students go off to write reviews for the books on their lists.

We spend the next work periods drafting reviews. I hop from kid to kid offering praise and feedback. When I see a word choice or writing move a student has made that I think might be helpful to other writers in the room, I get the class's attention and share some of their peers' ideas.

Day Seven

Most kids have completed their lists by now, but I set aside this day for kids who need more support and time. We use this day to clean up presentations and add cover images to students' book lists, which have been created in Google Docs.

Before our next class together, I print a copy of each student's "Best Books..." list for our celebration. I also combine all the lists into one long document so I can print copies of the cumulative lists for every student and the classroom library. I'll staple or bind this collection of book lists for kids to take home as a resource for finding books going forward.

Our classroom library copy of this year's lists will go into sheet protectors in a one-inch binder. I select a student to create a cover for our book list collection that they feel best represents our reading community.

Day Eight: Celebration Day!

We hold our best book lists celebration in the library because it has more space for kids to move around. Kids spread out their "Best Books..." lists on the library tables, so their classmates can read them. With their to-read lists in hand, my fifth graders read each other's lists, consider their classmates' recommendations, and add any books that look intriguing to their reading plans. Once all the kids have had an opportunity to make it through their classmates' lists, we come together as a class and share all of the books that we added to our book lists. Kids share what book they want to read, who recommended it, and what interests them about the book.

The lists become a source for summer reading recommendations and mementos for Colby's students of their reading year together. Copies remain in the classroom library for Colby's students in years to come. These readers will influence future generations of readers through their lists and their heartfelt recommendations about the books they loved.

Setting the Stage for Summer Reading

As we mentioned in Chapter One, school libraries and classroom libraries often serve as the main sources of books for many young readers. That means some students lose their book access every year when school closes for the summer. Regardless of how much your students have grown as readers during the school year, without access to books, their skills may decline, and their motivation may fade away. Eighty percent of the reading achievement gap between students from middle-income homes and lower-income homes (who often have less access to books) occurs during the summer, and this loss is cumulative (Alexander, Entwisle, & Olson, 2007). It does not matter how fun the kickoff party or the prizes for the schoolwide summer reading program are if kids don't have any books to read. A schoolwide effort is essential to ensure they have books to read all summer, considering that reading at home is the only activity that leads to learning gains in the summer, according to research (Kim & Quinn, 2013). Kids need to read over the summer, but they can't do it without books.

Book donation programs, long-term loans from the school library, and community book drives can increase students' access to books and raise awareness for the importance of access. Work with local businesses and nonprofit organizations to fund bookmobiles and Little Free Libraries. Partner with your public library to sign up families for library cards. Ensure that students who need assistive technology to access books have it, along with the training and support they need to use it.

Your encouragement for students' reading lives, as well as your efforts to support them in developing agency as readers, will do more to keep students reading in the summer than a summer reading party. Because of your good teaching during the school year, your students have reading plans. They can locate books for themselves. They have the confidence that comes from knowing more about books and themselves as readers than ever before. The classroom library is no longer available to them, but the access they have had to it and the time they have spent in it will sustain them going forward.

After many years teaching high school students, teacher and author Penny Kittle currently works with college students. Many of them have been successful in K–12 school but are not able to keep up with the heavy reading and writing expectations in college. Talking with her students, Penny sees how many of them have not been connected to reading or books in years—if ever. Unfortunately, teachers' biases about what secondary students should read (or not) lead to kids fake-reading assigned texts and rarely reading books of their choice.

Helping Kids Find Themselves as Readers

Penny Kittle

Colby: Penny, what have you learned about classroom libraries through your work?

Penny: There's a lot of bias from educators around particular kinds of books like graphic novels. Our Book Love Foundation grant recipients get a lot of pushback in high school over graphic novels. They try to make the case for graphic novels. No matter what they're trying to support, they get a lot of pushback from colleagues and administrators. We all hold a bias against something, and the only way we break that is to start reading. That is one topic that I thought we would have broken by now.

Another misguided idea is that there are particular authors and books that kids need to read to be prepared for college. One of the problems is that so many teachers are products of an Honors English class. Some English teachers believe classic books are valuable because they read them, and they think that other kids will find them valuable. So many of the new teachers I have worked with have said, "I didn't sit in class with kids who didn't read these books." Well, you did, but they camouflaged fake-reading well.

I've learned how much courage teachers have when they believe something matters. They are fighting for it every day. They see the obstacles (to diversifying their collections and promoting current books). They go right past them and stand their ground. And they say, all kids deserve to find themselves as readers here in my classroom. All kids deserve a chance to find a flood of books that interest them.

Donalyn: It's all about access, right? It's more than just the physical access piece. If you don't have a tangible book to read—paper, ebook, audiobook—no reading is going to take place. Then you have social and cultural access and intellectual access, which goes beyond giving kids a book. It's about giving them access to the world of ideas, the world of human voices and experiences. So, adults are limiting access in multiple ways.

Penny: One of my students at UNH once wrote, "There are answers to questions I didn't even know I was asking." I had that quote over my classroom library for years. That is the piece of your own intellectual curiosity that has not had a chance to develop. Another student said to me, "You know, Ms. Kittle, I never understood #BlackLivesMatter. I didn't know what was happening until I read *Dear Martin* (by Nic Stone)." He wasn't curious enough to go find out when he was younger. He said, "I don't understand why I couldn't have read this in high school. I could have read this years ago. I wanted to know, but I didn't know what to ask, and I didn't know how to find out."

We haven't allowed kids to build up stamina because we keep handing them stuff that we know they're not going to read. As a result, they don't develop the stamina to take on something they are truly interested in learning. And he had to work at that. Kids who engage in ideas through a long study—sustained engagement over time—with an issue (like immigration, for example) are going to change the way they hear the news and the way they think. We're denying them that chance. It's a lovely moment when kids realize they're making these shifts in their own personal identities as readers continually throughout the year, and hopefully throughout their school years.

As we remind ourselves often, the goal of all teaching is independence. What are we teaching kids about reading that carries them forward? How can the short time we spend with them make a difference in their reading interest and identity? The scaffolding, access, and community a classroom library offers helps kids discover and develop an independent, engaged reading life.

TIME TO REFLECT

- **Talk with students to identify barriers to book access they have when they're away from school.** How can your school community support students who need access to books, as well as assistive technology? What do students need to remain engaged readers over the summer?

- **What interactions around and conversations about books and reading do you observe between students?** How can you foster those relationships? Offer one additional opportunity a week for students to talk with each other about their books. Reflect on what works best for your students—book-talking, informal partner chats, book passes, and so on.

TIME-TO-REFLECT QUESTIONS

Chapter 1: Giving Kids Books in the Classroom—and Beyond

- **How have you experienced book floods and book deserts in your life?** Did you own books as a child? Did you have a library card? How has your book access changed over your lifetime?

- **What about your students?** How does book access vary among them? What sources for reading material do they have beyond your classroom? Your school?

- **What resources does your public library offer?** What are the requirements for acquiring a library card and borrowing materials? What are the fine and fee policies? What barriers do you see to public library use?

Chapter Two: Building the Collection and Organizing the Library Space

- **Work with a colleague to MUSTIE one section of your classroom library, such as one bookcase or one genre.** What sorts of books did you remove? What books were you reluctant to part with? Why? What surprised you about the books you weeded? Partner with a grade-level colleague and help each other weed. What did your colleague notice about the books in your library that you missed?

- **Now use one of the culturally responsive evaluation resources we recommended on page 62, such as Teaching for Change's Guide to Selecting Anti-Bias Children's Books.** What did you discover about the representation in your classroom library? What gaps do you see in your collection now? Whose voices are missing? How has your weeding and evaluation activities influenced your priorities for text selection? What are your priorities now, and why?

Chapter Three: Introducing the Classroom Library to Students

- **What rituals and routines do you rely on to provide a variety of literacy experiences for students and support a classroom culture of reading?** What would you change about those rituals and routines? After reading this chapter, what are you interested in trying out or tweaking?

- **Select five students who would benefit from more support with book selection.** Create preview stacks of three to five books for each one of them. Use resources such as book lists and your school librarian to choose books for each stack. Confer with students and walk them through their preview stacks. What do you notice about students' previewing and evaluating strategies? Could each student find a book to read?

- **Consider your book-talking routines.** How can you leverage them to increase students' reading interest for books they avoid or unfamiliar books? What sections of the library need more book love? Select a book or two from genres students avoid or areas of the library they don't frequent. Did any students show interest? What did they think of the book or section after giving it a try? What types of readers do they think would appreciate the book? Why?

Chapter Four: Responding to Students' Needs and Interests

- **Talk with students to identify barriers to book access when they're away from school.** How can your school community support students who need access to books and/or assistive technology? What do students need to remain engaged readers over the summer?

- **What interactions around and conversations about books and reading do you observe between students?** How can you foster those relationships? Offer one additional opportunity a week for students to talk with each other about their books. Reflect on what works best for your students—book-talking, informal partner chats, book passes, and so on.

REFERENCES

Ahmed, S. K. (2018). *Being the change: Lessons and strategies to teach social comprehension.* Heinemann.

Alexander, K. L., Entwisle, D. R., & Olson, L. S. (2007). Lasting consequences of the summer learning gap. *American Sociological Review, 72*(2), 167–180. doi.org/10.1177/000312240707200202

Allen, J. (2000). *Yellow brick roads: Shared and guided paths to independent reading 4–12.* Stenhouse Publishers.

Allington, R. L. (2013). What really matters when working with struggling readers. *The Reading Teacher, 66*(7), 2013, pp. 520–530.

Beck, I. L., & McKeown, M. G. (2000, November 30). *Text talk: Capturing the benefits of read-aloud experiences for young children. The Reading Teacher, 55*(1) pp. 10–20. Retrieved March 11, 2022, from eric.ed.gov/?id=EJ632232

Bishop, R. S. (1990). Mirrors, windows, and sliding glass doors. *Perspectives, 6*(3), ix–xi.

Blau, D. (2001). *The child care problem: An economic analysis.* Russell Sage Foundation.

Bridges, L. & Constantino, R. (2014). Reading, our beloved companion. In *Open a world of possible: Real stories about the joy and power of reading* (pp. 240–241). Scholastic.

Brooks, M. D., & Frankel, K. K. (2019). Authentic choice: A plan for independent reading in a restrictive instructional setting. *Journal of Adolescent & Adult Literacy, 62*(5), 574–577. doi:10.1002/JAAL.936

Cherry-Paul, S., & Johansen, D. (2019). *Breathing new life into book clubs: A practical guide for teachers.* Heinemann.

Clark, C., & Poulton, L. (2010, November 30). *Book ownership and its relation to reading enjoyment, attitudes, behaviour and attainment: Some findings from the National Literacy Trust First Annual Survey.* National Literacy Trust. Retrieved March 8, 2022, from eric.ed.gov/?id=ED521658

Derman-Sparks, L. (2013). *Guide for selecting anti-bias children's books.* Social Justice Books. Retrieved March 11, 2022, from socialjusticebooks.org/guide-for-selecting-anti-bias-childrens-books

Evans, M. D. R., Kelley, J., Sikora, J., & Treiman, D. J. (2010). Family scholarly culture and educational success: Books and schooling in 27 nations. *Research in Social Stratification and Mobility, 28*(2), 171–197. doi.org/10.1016/j.rssm.2010.01.002

Everett, C. (2017, November 22). *There is no diverse book.* ImagineLIT. Retrieved April 11, 2022, from http://www.imaginelit.com/news/2017/11/21/there-is-no-diverse-book

Faverio, M., & Perrin, A. (2022, February 2). *Three-in-ten Americans now read e-books.* Pew Research Center.

Guthrie, J. T., Wigfield, A., & VonSecker, C. (2000). Effects of integrated instruction on motivation and strategy use in reading. *Journal of Educational Psychology, 92*(2) (2000): 331.

Harris, E. A., & Alter, A. (2022). Book ban efforts spread across the U.S. *The New York Times*, 30 Jan. 2022, https://www.nytimes.com/2022/01/30/books/book-ban-us-schools.html.

Harvey, S., & Ward, A. (2017). *From striving to thriving: Why kids who read excel.* Scholastic.

Harvey, S., Ward, A., Hoddinott, M., & Carroll, S. (2021). *Intervention reinvention: A volume-based approach to reading success.* Scholastic.

Hiebert, E. H., & Reutzel, D. A. (2010). *Revisiting silent reading: New directions for teachers and researchers.* Web.

Hixenbaugh, M. (2022, February 1). Book banning in Texas schools: Titles are pulled off library shelves in record numbers. *NBCNews.com*, https://www.nbcnews.com/news/us-news/texas-books-race-sexuality-schools-rcna13886.

Hurst, S., & Griffity, P. (2014, November 30). Examining the effect of teacher read-aloud on adolescent attitudes and learning. *Middle Grades Research Journal.* Retrieved March 11, 2022, from eric.ed.gov/?id=EJ1144390

Johnson, A., & Parker, K. (2020, October 1). *Literacy as a tool for liberation.* ASCD. Retrieved March 11, 2022, from ascd.org/el/articles/literacy-as-a-tool-for-liberation

Johnson, D. R., Huffman, B. L., & Jasper, D. M. (2014). Changing race boundary perception by reading narrative fiction. *Basic and Applied Social Psychology, 36*(1), 83–90. doi.org/10.1080/01973533.2013.856791

Kidd, D. C., & Castano, E. (2013). Reading literary fiction improves theory of mind. *Science, 342*(6156), 377–380. doi.org/10.1126/science.1239918

Kim, J. S., & Quinn, D. M. (2013). The effects of summer reading on low-income children's literacy achievement from kindergarten to grade 8. *Review of Educational Research, 83*(3), 386–431. doi.org/10.3102/0034654313483906

Kluth, P., & Chandler-Olcott, K. (2008). *A land we can share: Teaching literacy to students with autism.* P.H. Brookes Pub.

Krashen, S. D. (2004). *The power of reading: Insights from research.* Libraries Unlimited.

Krashen, S. D. (2013). *Second language acquisition: Theories, applications, and some conjectures.* Cambridge University Press.

Lance, K. C., & Hofschire, L. (2012). (rep.). *Change in school librarian staffing linked with change in CSAP reading performance, 2005 to 2011.* Denver, CO: Library Research Services.

Lance, K. C., & Kachel, D. E. (2018). Why school librarians matter: What years of research tell us. *Phi Delta Kappan, 99*(7), pp. 15–20.

Lance, K. C., & Kachel, D. E. (2021). Perspectives on school librarian employment in the United States, 2009–10 to 2018–19. *SLIDE: The School Librarian Investigation—Decline or Evolution?*

Larrick, N. (1965, September 11). The all-white world of children's books. *The Saturday Review.*

Larson, J. (2021, March 12). *CREW: A weeding manual for modern libraries: TSLAC.* CREW: A Weeding Manual for Modern Libraries | TSLAC. Retrieved March 11, 2022, from tsl.texas.gov/ld/pubs/crew/index.html

LibraryScienceWiki. (2021, September 21). *Five laws of library science by Dr. S. R. Ranganathan.* Wikipedia For Library & Information Science. Retrieved March 11, 2022, from libraryscience wiki.com/2021/07/five-laws-of-library-science-s.html

McFarland, J., Hussar, B., Wang, X., Zhang, J., Wang, K., Rathbun, A., Barmer, A., Cataldi, E. F., & Mann, F. B. (2018). The condition of education 2018. NCES 2018–144. *National Center for Education Statistics.*

McKenna, M., & Kear, D. (1990). Measuring attitude toward reading: A new tool for teachers. *The Reading Teacher, 43*(9). 626–639. 10.1598/RT.43.8.3.

Makarechi, K. (2015, February 5). Langston Hughes's 1944 rebuke of a racist children's book could have been written today. *Vanity Fair.*

Mansor, A. N., Rasul, M. S., Rauf, R. A., & Koh, B. L. (2012). Developing and sustaining reading habit among teenagers. *The Asia-Pacific Education Researcher, 22*(4), 357–365. doi.org/10.1007/s40299-012-0017-1

Mapp, K. L., Carver, I., & Lander, J. (2017). *Powerful partnerships: A teacher's guide to engaging families for student success.* Scholastic.

Miller, D., & Kelley, S. (2013). *Reading in the wild: The book whisperer's keys to cultivating lifelong reading habits.* Jossey-Bass.

Miller, D., & Lesesne, T. S. (2022). *The joy of reading.* Heinemann.

Miller, D., & Sharp, C. (2018). *Game changer!: Book access for all kids.* Scholastic.

Muhammad, G. (2020). *Cultivating genius: An equity framework for culturally and historically responsive literacy.* Scholastic.

NAEP. (2005). *The nation's report card: Reading 2005.* NAEP—The Nation's Report Card: Reading 2005: Executive Summary. Retrieved March 8, 2022, from nces.ed.gov/nationsreportcard/pubs/main2005/2006451.aspx

Naidoo, J. C. (2014, April 5). *The importance of diversity in library programs and ...* American Library Association. Retrieved March 11, 2022, from ala.org/alsc/sites/ala.org.alsc/files/content/ALSCwhitepaper_importance%20of%20diversity_with%20graphics_FINAL.pdf

NCTE. (2017, May 31). *Statement on classroom libraries.* NCTE. Retrieved March 8, 2022, from ncte.org/statement/classroom-libraries

NCTE. (2019, November 7). *Independent reading.* NCTE. Retrieved March 11, 2022, from ncte.org/statement/independent-reading

NEA. (2007). *To read or not to read: A question of national consequence.* National Endowment for the Arts.

Neuman, S. B., & Celano, D. C. (2012). *Giving our children a fighting chance: Poverty, literacy, and the development of information capital.* Teachers College Press.

Neuman, S. B. and Knapczyk, J. J. (2018). Reaching families where they are: Examining an innovative book distribution program. *Urban Education, 55*(4), pp. 542–569.

Neuman, S. B., & Moland, N. (2016). Book deserts: The consequences of income segregation on children's access to print. *Urban Education, 54*(1), pp. 126–147. doi.org/10.1177/0042085916654525

Nystrand, M. (2006, April 30). *Research on the role of classroom discourse as it affects reading comprehension.* Research in the Teaching of English. Retrieved March 11, 2022, from eric.ed.gov/?id=EJ761632

Reading Is Fundamental (2010). Access to print materials improves children's reading. https://www.rif.org/sites/default/files/BFO_Research_OneSheet_v2.pdf

Reis, Sally M., D. McCoach, B., Coyne, M., Schreiber, F. J., Eckert, R. D., & Gubbins, E. J. (2007). Using planned enrichment strategies with direct instruction to improve reading fluency, comprehension, and attitude toward reading: An evidence-based study. *The Elementary School Journal, 108*(1), pp. 3–23.

Reutzel, D. R., & Fawson, P. C. (2002, April 1). *Changing the face of reading instruction: Recommendations ... Reading Horizons.* Retrieved March 11, 2022, from scholarworks.wmich.edu/cgi/viewcontent.cgi?referer=&httpsredir=1&article=1189&context=reading_horizons

Scholastic. (2019). *Kids & family reading report.* Retrieved March 11, 2022, from scholastic.com/readingreport/home.html

Shurr, J., & Taber-Doughty, T. (2012, August 31). *Increasing comprehension for middle school students with moderate intellectual disability on age-appropriate texts.* Education and Training in Autism and Developmental Disabilities. Retrieved March 11, 2022, from eric.ed.gov/?id=EJ986321

Tatum, A. W. (2009). *Reading for their life: (Re)building the textual lineages of African American adolescent males.* Heinemann.

Terry, Y., & Lance, K. C. (2016). *School libraries work!: A compendium of research supporting the effectiveness of school libraries.* Scholastic Library Publishing.

Varlas, L. (2018). *Why every class needs read alouds.* ASCD. Retrieved March 11, 2022, from ascd.org/el/articles/why-every-class-needs-read-alouds

Vu, D. (2021). *Life, literacy, and the pursuit of happiness: Supporting our immigrant and refugee children through the power of reading.* Scholastic.

Wong, A. (2016, July 14). The children who grow up in 'book deserts.' *The Atlantic.* Retrieved March 8, 2022, from theatlantic.com/education/archive/ 2016/07/where-books-are-nonexistent/491282

Yorio, K. (2018, April 3). Fighting cuts: How to keep librarians in schools. *School Library Journal.* Retrieved March 8, 2022, from slj.com/?detailStory=fighting-cuts-keep-librarians-schools

CONTRIBUTOR BIOS

Lynsey Burkins has worked for children for the past 18 years, creating antiracist spaces where they feel free, have agency, and know they are loved. She currently serves third-grade students and presents on topics that include using literature to help students make sense of their world and as a vehicle to nurture their spirits and minds. Lynsey has a forthcoming book, with Franki Sibberson, on whole-group reading instruction.

Becky Calzada is a first-generation Texas educator and the district library coordinator in Leander ISD, which is located northwest of Austin, Texas. She is a director-at-large for AASL, on the legislative committee for TxLA, past chair for the TxASL, and co-founder of #FReadom Fighters. Follow Becky on Twitter @becalzada.

Suzanne Carroll has served as Mamaroneck's RTI coordinator and literacy intervention coach since 2017. She has been an educator for 20 years, holding the positions of classroom teacher and literacy coach. She is coauthor of *Intervention Reinvention: A Volume-Based Approach to Reading Success.*

Maggie Hoddinott has served in a variety of leadership and teaching roles, including supervisor of elementary instruction, literacy ambassador, Reading Recovery teacher, and classroom teacher. Much of what Maggie has learned about matching children with compelling books is reflected in *Intervention Reinvention: A Volume-Based Approach to Reading Success,* which she co-authored with Stephanie Harvey, Annie Ward, and Suzanne Carroll.

Penny Kittle teaches writing at Plymouth State University in New Hampshire. She taught in public schools for 34 years and learned two essential things: all students will build independent reading lives of joy, curiosity, and hunger when given agency; and teachers who write *with* their students generate community and creative power. Penny is the founder of the Book Love Foundation. She has written nine books on teaching and travels the world to learn beside teachers and students.

Jennifer LaGarde is a lifelong teacher and learner, with over 20 years in public education. Her educational passions include leveraging technology to help students develop authentic reading lives and meeting the unique needs of students living in poverty. A huge fan of YA literature, Jennifer currently lives, works, reads, and drinks lots of coffee in Olympia, Washington. Follow her adventures at www.librarygirl.net.

Franki Sibberson, past-president of the National Council of Teachers of English (NCTE), is a literacy leader with 33 years of elementary classroom experience in Ohio. She is the co-author of several professional books, including *Beyond Leveled Books, Still Learning to Read*, and *Day-to-Day Assessment in the Reading Workshop*. Franki currently provides leadership and consulting to schools and nonprofits, supporting both local and national literacy initiatives.

Katherine Sokolowski has taught for more than 20 years, from kindergarten through seventh grade, and currently teaches seventh grade in Monticello, Illinois. Her thoughts about the power of relationships to engage readers and writers have appeared on NPR, in *Choice Literacy*, and in NCTE's *Voices from the Middle*. Katherine co-facilitates The Nerdy Book Club blog and also writes for the blog Read Write Reflect at readwriteandreflect.blogspot.com.

Don Vu has been an elementary school teacher and principal for 24 years. He spreads the message that literacy can change the world through his work with state and national literacy organizations. He is the author of *Life, Literacy, and the Pursuit of Happiness: Supporting Our Immigrant and Refugee Children Through the Power of Reading*. You can find out more at drdonvu.com.

Annie Ward has served as the assistant superintendent for curriculum and instruction for the Mamaroneck Public Schools in Westchester County, New York, since 2004. Prior to that, she was a local instructional superintendent for the New York City Department of Education and the Supervisor of Curriculum and Instruction for the Ridgewood, New Jersey, Public Schools. She is the author, with Stephanie Harvey, of *From Striving to Thriving: How to Grow Confident, Capable Readers*.

ACKNOWLEDGMENTS

It takes a lot of people to make a book. When creating a book about teaching, it takes a lot of kids and teachers—learning together. We would like to thank our students—former and present—for teaching us how classroom libraries can influence readers and shape a reading community. We are thankful for the caregivers and parents who gave permission for their children to appear in this book. We have been blessed to teach alongside incredible colleagues during our careers, and we are better teachers because we have learned with all of you.

Conducting the interviews for this book is a career highlight for both of us. We had the honor of learning from some of the best educators and reading advocates we know. Thank you Penny, Don, Katherine, Annie, Maggie, Suzanne, Becky, Franki, Lynsey, and Jennifer. We know that your advice and experiences have contributed something special to this book.

The two of us are grateful for our Nerdy Book Club collaborators, Cindy Minnich and Katherine Sokolowksi. They keep Nerdy running on a daily basis and work with all of our posters to prepare and publish content for the blog. Cindy and Katherine are also inspiring and talented teachers who have taught us a lot about encouraging middle and high schoolers to read more.

We appreciate the Scholastic team for their guidance and skill in creating this book. A special thanks to our developmental editor, Ray Coutu, who understood the vision we had for the book and helped us bring it to reality. We also thank Sarah Longhi, Tara Welty, Danny Miller, Shelley Griffin, Tannaz Fassihi, and Maria Lilja.

We appreciate our agent, Molly O'Neil, for her great advice and advocacy. The two of us will always be grateful for our mentor and friend, Lois Bridges, who invited us to write for Scholastic. Lois is now executive director of Bring Me a Book, working tirelessly to support kids' book access and promote best practices.

Donalyn: I would like to thank my husband, Don, for sharing my mission to increase children's reading engagement and access to books. He personally labeled and stamped most of my classroom library bins and books over the years! Don understands the importance of books and reading in his own life. He wants kids to have books, too. He handles almost every book that comes into or leaves our house. He never says a word when I buy more of them. If I have mailed you books, Don took them to the post office. The clerks call him The Book Man.

Colby: I would like to thank my wife, Alaina, and our five children for being supportive of the time creating this book took away from our family. I'd also like to thank Chris Kindy, whose work in the Lakeview Community School District helped me to see the importance and power of classroom libraries.

INDEX